EFFECTIVE SUPERVISION FOR COUNSELLORS: AN INTRODUCTION

HAZEL REID AND JANE WESTERGAARD

Series editor: Norman Claringbull

Los Angeles | London | New Delhi
Singapore | Washington DC

Learning Matters
An imprint of SAGE Publications Ltd
1 Oliver's Yard
55 City Road
London EC1Y 1SP

SAGE Publications Inc.
2455 Teller Road
Thousand Oaks, California 91320

SAGE Publications India Pvt Ltd
B 1/I 1 Mohan Cooperative Industrial Area
Mathura Road
New Delhi 110 044

SAGE Publications Asia-Pacific Pte Ltd
3 Church Street
#10–04 Samsung Hub
Singapore 049483

Editor: Luke Block
Development editor: Lauren Simpson
Production controller: Chris Marke
Project management: Diana Chambers
Marketing manager: Tamara Navaratnam
Cover design: Wendy Scott
Typeset by: Kelly Winter
Printed by: MPG Printgroup, UK

Library of Congress Control Number:
2012955074

British Library Cataloguing in Publication
Data

A catalogue record for this book is available
from the British Library

ISBN 978 1 44625 713 5
ISBN 978 1 44625 455 4 (pbk)

Contents

Series Editor's Preface

The study of counselling and psychotherapy is mostly about the study of relationships. After all, most therapists would probably agree that therapeutic practice is mostly about the use of relationships to facilitate change. This is why so much of practitioner training and professional activity focuses on the exploration of the therapist/client relationship. This relationship is fundamental; it is at the core of the psychological therapies. However, there is another relationship that is vital – mandatory even – in the professional practice of counselling and psychotherapy. Many clients are unaware that it even exists. It is the relationship between therapists and their clinical supervisors. This relationship is considered to be so important that all counsellors and psychotherapists are encouraged to routinely and regularly interact and consult with their supervisors throughout their professional lives. Indeed, all the professionally accrediting bodies demand proof of ongoing supervision as part of their admissions systems and ongoing professional development programmes.

It can be argued that the practitioner/supervisor relationship lies at the heart of responsible and effective counselling and psychotherapy. That is why books like this one are so central to therapist development and therapeutic practice. Hazel Reid and Jane Westergaard are experienced and competent counselling teachers and theorists. Already enjoying a well-deserved reputation as authoritative writers about counselling, they have used their expertise profitably in this book to offer us a fresh overall perspective on the supervision process. The key to Jane and Hazel's approach is interactivity. They firmly position the therapist/supervisor relationship as a two-way street. Both participants are responsible for this relationship's direction and its outcomes; both participants benefit from the learning gained.

From the very beginning of the book, Jane and Hazel make it clear that supervision is a collaborative process with both participants responsible for its management. This notion that both supervisee and supervisor have equality of purpose and accountability might be a difficult idea for trainee counsellors and psychotherapists to take on board. However, as Jane and Hazel point out, a vital element in practitioner maturation is the growing ability of therapists to take personal responsibility for their own professional decisions and standards; to develop their own 'inner supervisor'. Speaking as a counselling and psychotherapy teacher myself, I always feel that my teaching has been successful when my students have become confident enough to declare that they have 'outgrown' their supervisors. Of course, that does not mean that they have outgrown supervision. It just means that they now have different supervisory needs. They are ready to manage their supervision in different ways, to go in different directions, and to work with different supervisors.

Having established the vital role that the active supervisee plays in the supervision process, Jane and Hazel go on to examine the supervisors' responsibilities too. Good supervision not only requires active supervisees, it also requires active and well-trained supervisors as well.

Like therapy itself, supervision is a very broad church with many varying styles, approaches and underpinning theories. Jane and Hazel explore these various concepts and offer guidance on how to manage a bewildering array of supervisory choices. This book informs us that, just like good quality counselling or well-targeted psychotherapy, supervision at its best is a transformatory process that is continually evolving.

This is an excellent 'hands on' book that will be of enormous help to supervisors and supervisees alike. It offers a 'step-by-step' guide that shows us how to build the supervisory relationship (from both sides) and how to ensure that relationship matures over time. At its heart, this book shows supervisors and supervisees how to get the best out of their working relationships. This book is full of useful exercises, practical hints, case studies and lots of guidance about future learning.

Anybody with an interest in the counselling and psychotherapy 'business' will gain a lot from reading this book. I wholeheartedly recommend it to students, practitioners, teachers, managers and supervisors alike. Jane and Hazel are excellent teachers who write in an accessible and user-friendly way.

Dr Norman Claringbull – Series Editor
www.normanclaringbull.co.uk

Acknowledgements

Many thanks to Lauren, Luke, Norman and the team at Sage/Learning Matters for their encouragement and support.

About the authors

Hazel Reid is a Reader in Career Guidance and Counselling, and Director of the Centre for Career and Personal Development at Canterbury Christ Church University, UK. She teaches career counselling theory and research methods, and supervises a number of students undertaking doctoral research. She has a particular interest in reflexive, narrative and biographic approaches in research that is related to education and the 'helping' services. Hazel is a Fellow of the Institute of Career Guidance and a Fellow of the National Institute for Career Education and Counselling. She has published widely and presents her work at national and international conferences. She is involved in European projects connected to the work of career and school counsellors. Her previous research was concerned with the meanings given to the function of supervision within career counselling and youth support work. Currently she is exploring the development of constructivist approaches for integrative career counselling.

Jane Westergaard is a senior lecturer at Canterbury Christ Church University, UK. She teaches on a range of programmes specifically designed for students who plan to work with young people in a range of settings, but not in teaching roles. These youth support professionals include school counsellors, classroom assistants, learning mentors, careers advisers and personal advisers. Jane has a particular interest in counselling young people, working with young people in the group context and supervision. She has recently published a book, *Effective Group Work with Young People*. Jane has spoken on the subjects of counselling, supervision and group work at a number of national and international conferences. She is a qualified and practising UKRC registered counsellor, working with young people and adult clients.

Introduction

Hazel Reid

In 2011, Jane and I were invited to a party – an authors' party to celebrate the establishment of Learning Matters as part of Sage Publications. It was in the winter, in the week, in the evening and in a busy work period for us both. However, we had enjoyed writing our previous book with Learning Matters, had been treated very well and felt some obligation to attend. We had also been asked to write a second book on supervision for the same Learning Matters series *Counselling & Psychotherapy Practice*. So, on the feeble basis of 'I'll go if you will', we met in the lobby of an attractive building near the rejuvenated King's Cross area of London. It was a very pleasant event, quietly celebratory, and we spoke to a number of interesting people. One of those interesting people we met for the first time was Windy Dryden, a distinguished counsellor, academic and author who has been writing and editing for Sage for many years. When he learned that we were writing a book on supervision he asked: 'Why, when there are so many out there already? How will yours be different?'

Jane and I did not have a ready answer, but it was, and is, an important question. I hope we said something plausible in reply (I cannot remember). Windy remained resolutely charming as we moved on to other topics, but the question haunted me rather. I worry about reductionism, about 'surface-layer' writing. I get anxious about accusations of providing simplistic explanations that ignore the subtleties that an in-depth exploration would provide. And then Jane will admonish me thus: *But we have been asked to write an 'introduction to supervision' – not a supervision handbook or a comprehensive explanation of a particular approach to supervision. By its very nature it has to summarise, but the breadth can lead the reader to examine the depth in the references we draw on and the suggested reading lists we will provide.* She's right, of course, but how should I answer Windy's question? Why are we writing it and what might make this book different?

An honest answer to the first part of that question would be 'because we were asked to' – and there's nothing wrong with a bit of healthy narcissism! We also have a sustained interest in the topic. My doctoral work was researching career counsellors', their line managers' and the profession's understandings of the purpose and functions of supervision. Currently, my supervision is of doctoral students in a faculty of education, and the knowledge and skills gained from researching counselling supervision are vital for this learning work to be effective and collaborative. Jane is a qualified and practising UKRC registered counsellor with over 20 years' engagement in supervision. Her recent research explored the experience of supervisors who were supervising colleagues that they also line-managed.

A more serious answer would be that any book series on counselling would not be complete without a title that focuses on supervision. Supervision is an integral aspect of counselling practice in the UK: indeed, the British Association for Counselling & Psychotherapy requires counsellors to receive clearly specified amounts of supervision. So, the book aims to introduce both 'new' and 'in-training' counsellors to the concept of supervision and its purpose within counselling – this is its rationale. It will also be useful for experienced counsellors who are undertaking supervision for the first time, or for those who wish to refresh their understanding of the practice. Like all the books in the series, it is written in a style that ensures accessibility for the intended audience, balancing insight into the underpinning theories and concepts with practical examples, case studies and activities. Like supervision, the place the book seeks to occupy is a learning space – showing rather than telling. It focuses on key elements of supervision, including functions, methods and models, ethics, processes and skills, and examines in depth the supervisory relationship. It also raises critical questions about the practice, and advocates flexibility and creativity, outlining alternative approaches alongside those that are tried and tested.

We are cognisant of the historical development of psychoanalysis, psychotherapy, counselling and the broader work of the helping professions, and we are aware of the confusion caused by the terms. With the exception of psychiatry (which requires a medical qualification) the boundaries between the above are not always clear. In current practice many therapists will cross boundaries in their work, using methods from approaches other than those they were schooled in during their initial training (Claringbull, 2010). In terms of supervision, all professionals who are involved in counselling people with emotional, psychological and other mental health 'problems' benefit from supervision. As a generic title, then, we will use the term 'counsellor' in this book.

The writing style is personal and informal, although the content is grounded in theory. We use first-person pronouns in the desire to produce work that is interactive and engaging. We draw on our teaching in, and our research on, supervision. Our examples and case studies in the book are based on our experience, but, unless they state they are quotes from our research, they are 'fictions' designed to illustrate a point made in the text. This does not make the stories told less meaningful: we hope they have an explanatory power that illuminates the page. This practice is shared in many other texts, and the majority of those we recommend use case studies, drawing from the personal experience of the authors. Like the books it cites, *Effective Supervision for Counsellors: An Introduction* will retain its relevance as it is not envisaged that supervision will cease to be important in the UK, and the importance of supervision may increase in other countries where counselling is an established or developing practice. Although failing to answer Windy's question in full, we will justify our text as a useful addition to the range – one that will introduce the reader to the breadth of literature on the practice, building on the strengths of the Learning Matters/Sage series.

CHAPTER CONTENTS

The book is written with a certain logical progress, but we are mindful that readers will choose their own pathway through the material. As we developed our thinking about the content, it became apparent that the book fell into two halves, the first half being concerned with general principles and explanations, and the second with the phase-by-phase development of the supervisory relationship. There is some overlap in places where, for example, a concept is introduced in the first part and then developed more fully in the context of the supervisory relationship that is explored in the second part. This is not a problem – it should assist the reader. The final chapter in the book considers the support needs of supervisors and discusses strategies for dealing with issues encountered in supervisory practice. It also reflects on the place of research in continuing professional development.

Part One: Key theories and concepts

In Chapter 1, 'What is supervision?', counselling supervision is defined, drawing on the literature from a range of counselling contexts. The purpose and functions of supervision are discussed in this opening chapter. Alongside defining what it is, the chapter also explores ideas about the giving and receiving of supervision, reflecting on what is meant by providing a 'safe space' for effective and reflexive supervision. To illustrate the discussion a research case study is drawn on, where practitioners were asked to give their views about the practice and practicalities of supervision. The various issues raised are explored in later chapters in the book.

A number of general concepts that are central in counselling practice are just as important in supervision, and are discussed in Chapter 2, 'The ethical counsellor and supervision'. These concepts include understanding ethical principles in context, working towards multicultural and anti-oppressive practice, the links between ethical behaviour and reflexivity, and how personal values have an impact on supervision. Chapter 3, 'Theoretical frameworks for supervision', considers theoretical models that have been developed for, or are applicable to, supervision. The theories that are explored provide 'tools to think with' that can help to frame supervisory practice. Descriptions of developmental and process models are given, and these are followed by an introduction to aspects from cognitive behavioural, solution focused and narrative counselling that can be applied in supervision. This leads on to a discussion about the value of integrated approaches in supervision, before exploring key concepts from Gestalt and psychodynamic therapy.

Chapter 4, 'Methods for giving and receiving supervision', reviews how we organise supervision. It explores individual, group and other variations for the giving and receiving of supervision, including supervision 'at a distance' and self-supervision. The advantages and disadvantages of each are considered, alongside examining creative possibilities for the development of supervisory practice. The chapter introduces a cautionary note into the discussion, reminding the reader that reflexive practice also requires us to be critical thinkers, questioning what we do, and why and how we do it.

Part Two: Charting the development of the supervisory relationship

Chapter 5, 'Preparing for supervision', is the first chapter in the second part of the book, which maps the development of the supervisory relationship through the five phases of:

1 preparing;
2 establishing;
3 progressing;
4 working at depth;
5 ending.

Chapter 5 identifies what needs to happen *before* the supervisory relationship is established – the preparation phase. Building on the previous chapters, it clarifies the responsibilities of both supervisor and supervisee, and covers the essential aspects for effective planning that also take into account the many practical issues. Three characters are introduced, and their progress is followed in the four subsequent chapters. As each case study develops, the reader is invited to examine the effectiveness of the supervisory relationship.

With the 'groundwork' covered in Chapter 5, Chapter 6, 'Establishing an effective supervisory relationship', clarifies what needs to happen in the first supervisory session. It examines the features that exemplify an effective supervisory relationship, considering the core conditions of a person-centred approach. It gives particular importance to agreeing a contract for supervision, which is necessary for establishing an effective working agreement. Moving on, Chapter 7, 'Progressing the supervisory relationship', takes further the examination of the main theories and concepts that were introduced in Chapter 3 and applies them to practice. In addition it explores the key principles of transactional analysis as a means of understanding communication and miscommunication in the supervisory relationship.

Chapter 8, 'Maintaining a working alliance in supervision', moves to the next phase in the relationship, where supervisor and supervisee are 'working at depth'. The maintenance of the working alliance is studied, drawing on the skills of immediacy and challenge – central to sustaining an effective supervisory relationship. In the process of reviewing the relationship, the chapter examines the notion of the 'inner supervisor' and the need for creativity, incorporating creative and narrative approaches. Chapter 9, 'Moving on – ending the supervisory relationship', brings us to the last phase, but as the title suggests this is described as a beginning also: a moving on to new relationships. Although the chapter discusses how to manage endings effectively, it returns us to the core concept that supervision is a process, not a linear event with a start and a finish. Yet endings also herald a need for evaluation – on the relationship and the processes. In this chapter we review the supervisory case studies that have been followed through Chapters 5 to 9.

Chapter 10, 'Supervising the supervisor – transforming counselling practice', is the final chapter. While the second part of the book has focused on the development of the relationship between the supervisor and the supervisee, the closing chapter considers the issues that supervisors may face and their support needs. It also discusses the possibilities for dissemination of supervisory practice through research into what can and should be a transformative process. To illustrate this last point, it examines findings from a recent project that Jane has undertaken with supervisors – researching views about line-manager supervision.

Reading, thinking, discussing and drafting ideas, developing the writing, giving and receiving feedback on the chapters: these activities amount to a learning process, as is supervision. Sometimes the thoughts flowed into words and at other times the words were struggled over, tried out, reshaped or discarded. I love reading, but I write to understand and it is often the development of the case studies or the structuring of an activity that enhances my understanding. The creation of this book has, overall, been enjoyable, in large part because Jane and I know we will work well together and keep to our contract for writing. We prepare well, we are both organised people, but it is more than that; as in effective supervision, we have an established relationship built on trust and mutual respect that we nurture in our writing partnership. We trust that you will find equally good relationships in your supervisory experiences and we hope that this book helps.

SUGGESTED FURTHER READING

Claringbull, N (2010) *What is counselling & psychotherapy?* Exeter: Learning Matters.

This is an accessible text that gives a clear overview of the counselling profession, charting its antecedents and expansion alongside current developments.

PART ONE

KEY THEORIES AND CONCEPTS

CHAPTER 1

What is supervision?

Hazel Reid

CORE KNOWLEDGE

This chapter will provide the opportunity to:

- consider definitions on the purpose and functions of supervision;
- explore ideas about the giving and receiving of supervision;
- reflect on the concept of a 'safe space' for effective supervisory practice.

INTRODUCTION

> *Supervision is a collaborative process in which the supervisor works with the supervisee to explore their work reflectively . . . Fundamental to the relationship is good rapport and a working alliance.*
> (Schuck and Wood, 2011, p15)

There are a number of words in the above quote that are key to our understanding of the practice of effective supervision within counselling: these are 'collaborative', 'reflectively', 'relationship', 'rapport' and 'a working alliance'. In order to identify the purpose and functions of supervision, this chapter considers a number of definitions that are drawn from the literature across a range of professional contexts and that encompass these key words and terms. The terms themselves are examined more fully as we progress through the book, but starting with general definitions about supervision seems sensible. The chapter also discusses who receives supervision, who 'gives' it, who wants it and if it is necessary at all. In other words, should supervision be a requirement for all counsellors all the time, or are there differing views about this? The location where supervision takes place is an important consideration, and the requirement for a 'safe space' for effective supervision is also explored.

Before turning to the literature for definitions on the purpose and functions of supervision, we look at a sample of the reflections of practitioners gathered in a case study for a research project (Reid, 2010). These eleven practitioners worked in youth support and were undertaking a certificated programme to develop their role as supervisors. In the research case study below, they are discussing their experiences of both receiving and giving supervision. These reflections highlight a number of wide-ranging issues that are discussed within the book.

Case study 1.1 What are your thoughts about the practice and practicalities of supervision?

All the participants who took part in the research case study saw the purpose of supervision as providing an opportunity to discuss caseloads, particular clients and issues that arose in the work, and to develop their practice alongside an opportunity to attend to self-care: their support needs. This was summed up by one participant, who said:

> *Support needs are paramount, having the time and space to talk through difficult situations enables practitioners to function effectively, this in turn helps and supports clients.*

Another, reflecting on what supervision was not, made reference to the boundaries within supervision. She indicated that too much focus on support needs can lead the supervisor into taking a counselling role:

> *There is a danger that some of the issues being addressed could overstep the boundaries in terms of the supervisor becoming the counsellor, which I would feel very uncomfortable with.*

In stressing their views about the importance of supervision for their practice to remain effective, a major issue that they all raised was the allocation and effective use of time for supervision. Participants said that the effective use of this time is at risk when *workloads and deadlines constantly clash*. On this tension, one participant stated:

> *The busier someone is the more important it is for them to have space and time for reflection and support – to continue to be effective.*

The participants in this group expressed a preference for one-to-one supervision over group supervision as they were *more likely to set aside time and carry out the necessary effective work*. Another participant added: *Trying to get a mutually suitable time for groups has been very difficult and, in my experience, has meant most groups have failed.*

They also talked about the importance of preparation by both supervisor and supervisee and of the sessions following a pattern or structure. Other comments were made about the location of supervision in order to manage the time effectively, for example, *in a private place without distractions.*

Summing up their views on what supervision had done for them, one practitioner in the group felt supervision had made little difference to their practice, but the other ten all responded differently to this. They claimed it had enhanced their work, leading to greater reflective practice, and had promoted sharing of good practice. It had been *invaluable for sanity, professional integrity and effectiveness*, had given *confidence and ensured a safer working environment*, and had promoted *competence and evaluative practice – leading to greater autonomy*.

One participant wished to emphasise the importance of training for the role of supervisor. Another described supervision as giving them *permission to reflect fully, knowing that whatever issues I unearth, there is somewhere to take them*. Finally, one practitioner made the following comment:

> *Supervision has helped me to develop my practice further – it has been an enabling process and has supported me to identify, accept and develop personal areas for development as a practitioner.*

Having heard the voices of practitioners, we will now consider definitions from the literature on the purpose and functions of supervision.

THE PURPOSE OF SUPERVISION

While the literature will encompass the words emphasised earlier – i.e. collaborative, working reflectively, relationship, rapport and a working alliance – the literature from a number of helping services, including counselling, may indicate differences in emphasis on the purpose of supervision (i.e. what it tries to achieve). The exploration here will concentrate on the definitions within counselling, but across many sectors the aim is to highlight the importance of creating a reflective space for enhancing the work. As a fundamental component of supervision, it might be useful to explore the meaning of reflectivity as a first step.

ACTIVITY 1.1 DEFINING REFLECTIVITY AND REFLEXIVITY

Reflective practice is a term that you are likely to be familiar with, but can you define it succinctly in a couple of sentences? Try doing this now – without reading what follows – and write it down.

You may also have encountered the term reflexivity in your reading and practice – how is this different to reflectivity? Again, try to define this term.

Reflexivity within supervision is considered in more detail in the next chapter as part of ethical practice, but before moving on, how do your definitions compare with the following suggestions?

A reflective practitioner is someone who is able to reach potential solutions through analysing experience and prior knowledge in order to inform current and future practice. The internal process of reflection that is active and conscious could be described as reflectivity. Reflexivity is the process by which we are aware of our own responses to what is happening in a particular context (i.e. a counselling interaction) and our reactions to people, events and the dialogue taking place. A reflexive understanding will include an awareness of the personal, social and cultural context and its influence on both the speaker and the listener. Reflexive awareness in counselling practice leads to a deeper understanding of how we co-construct knowledge about the world and ways of operating within it that are more meaningful for those involved.

Returning to definitions of supervision within counselling, Bradley et al. (2001) discuss purpose via the principles, process and practice of supervision. Supervision can be divided into two words, 'super' and 'vision'. In other words, the experienced person looks from above (super) on the work of a less experienced person and has a view (vision) of the work. This resonates with Hawkins and Shohet's statement (1989, p37) that a supervisor requires 'helicopter ability' – i.e. the ability both to move in close and to pull away to get a broader perspective. For a beginner supervisor, no matter how experienced as a practitioner, that can be difficult to accomplish when trying to keep in balance a number of sometimes competing goals within the practice of supervision (Wiener et al., 2003). Supervision, like counselling, is a complicated process – more complex, perhaps, as the supervisor does not work directly with the client and the supervisee selects what to 'bring' to supervision. In their more recent work, Hawkins and Shohet (2006) stress the collaborative nature of the work and emphasise the importance of encouraging a learning culture in the practice of supervision.

Holloway and Aposhyan (1994) define supervision for trainee counsellors as the means both to acquire the necessary knowledge and skills for effective practice and to engage in a learning climate that enables them to experience their *own interpersonal power* (p194). To accomplish this, the supervisor takes on the roles of 'teacher', model and mentor. Harris and Brockbank (2011) pay particular attention to the place of learning theory within their integrative approach, which has been developed for both new and experienced therapists and supervisors. The suggestion is that supervisors need to examine the working context and their own experience of supervision, identifying the learned philosophy and potential bias in their own supervisory practice. In other words, are they making assumptions about the universality of the approach they use based on what they received in their own supervision, or are they open to critiquing this and trying different methods? As Harris and Brockbank state (2011, p57), without this reflexivity, *the implicit model is passed on to the supervisee, without the supervisor being aware of it*. What is emphasised here is that supervision takes place within a learning climate where participants are prepared to learn and work collaboratively.

REFLECTION POINT

In a similar way to Harris and Brockbank, this book takes an integrative approach to supervision, but what is your view about an integrative approach? What is the counselling orientation that shapes your practice? What might be the implications for you if, for example, you were supervising a counsellor whose theoretical and practical approach differed from yours?

Dryden et al. (1995) highlight the difficulties where supervisor and supervisee may have been trained within different theoretical models of counselling. An argument could be made that exploring the differences can help us to question our assumptions and ensure meanings are shared in what should be a collaborative process. But that might ignore the realities of what happens in practice, and this highlights the importance of considering the theoretical perspectives that inform the work of both supervisor and supervisee at, or even before, the contracting stage of the work.

One of the requirements of an effective supervisor is to be open to challenge, to refrain from an expert stance and to be able to live with uncertainty and negative capability – and to learn from the experience. This is not about incompetence, but being in a position of not knowing may make us feel uncomfortable and not in control. Gallwey expresses this as a *willingness to be a beginner*:

> *The willingness to be a beginner is an essential ingredient to being a good learner – no matter what your level of expertise. It is the willingness to 'not know' and to be comfortable with not knowing that makes children and adults able to learn without fear.*

> *The purpose and functions of supervision will differ according to the context in which counsellors are working and the groups and/or individuals they work with. These differences may also reflect whether they are in training, experienced, working in private practice or within a public service; and will also be influenced by whether participation is compulsory or voluntary.*
> (cited in Hawkins and Shohet, 2006, p17)

In answering the question 'What is supervision?' Harris and Brockbank draw on the work of a number of writers (see Harris and Brockbank, 2011, p153) and list the descriptions given for supervision. These include: support, a series of tasks, a developmental process, training, a consultative process, a reflective process, an interpersonal interaction, an impossible profession, keepers of the faith (they suggest the last one is a bit grand!).

There is general agreement about what supervision is not, i.e. it is not therapy. Like one of the participants in the research case study above, most writers would separate supervision from therapy. Wiener et al. (2003) and Harris and Brockbank (2011) give useful overviews of the historical development of supervision and its separation from therapeutic analysis, but the boundaries may not be as clear as we think. Experience of personal counselling may be a requirement for counsellors in training, and this will be a practice separate from supervision – but if the supervision process is truly engaging, collaborative and developmental, it is likely to have therapeutic effects. As stated earlier, supervision is a relationship, and it is not a straightforward process.

REFLECTION POINT

What do you think? Are the two practices (personal counselling as a practitioner and supervision as a counsellor) distinct? If so, how? If there are therapeutic effects, what might these be? Could you list them?

Knight, writing about the therapist–supervisor relationship within clinical settings, says the following:

> *In the world of analysis, psychotherapy and casework, supervision has evolved from its original meaning of over-seeing and controlling, although there is an element of 'watching with authority over a process'. A context of enablement and support and the facilitation of learning from experience has developed with the personal engagement between supervisor and supervisee. It is a cooperative activity between an analyst or a student analyst with a supervisor who can bring to this meeting a view of the work with the patient untrammelled by direct emotional involvement. However, emotional involvement, transference both to the supervisee and to the patient, is inevitably evoked in the supervisor.*

(Knight, 2003, p35)

It seems that it is the supervisor's separation or distance from the client that enables the supervisee to reflect on the work. This space provides an opportunity for the supervisee to discuss difficulties with the work and its emotional involvement.

How that effective relationship is achieved in practice (as well as a discussion about transference and counter-transference) will be the focus of later chapters in this book. For now, a case study may help to illustrate the point about supervisory 'distance'.

Case study 1.2 Trainee counsellor Jan and supervisor Joseph

Jan (sounding frustrated): *I have this client who is really difficult to work with and I'm not sure really why. She always turns up, is on time and appears to engage with the sessions, but I don't know, we don't seem to get anywhere!*

Joseph: *Tell me a bit more about what you mean by 'we don't seem to get anywhere'.*

Jan: *Well, we have been working together now for six weeks and we still seem to be at the very beginning, not moving forward.*

Joseph: *Can you say something about where you think you should be together, in terms of moving forward?*

Jan: *Oh, I don't know. (sigh) Hearing myself say that, it sounds unreasonable.*

Joseph: *OK, I can hear that you feel both frustrated and confused by this – am I right?*

Jan: *Yes I am – I feel stuck.*

Joseph: *Well, let's go back a bit, Jan, and explore the start of the relationship then – the beginning. Of course, I have not met your client. Telling me about her might help us to think about what is happening, so that we can explore this stuckness – what do you think?*

Jan: *Yeah, it might help me to review why I feel a bit hopeless with this client.*

Joseph: *Right, so tell me the story of how you met and started to work with this client. I'll try not to interrupt, unless I think a question may help us to focus our thinking better.*

In the case study what Joseph refrains from doing is to offer solutions or techniques. He recognises the emotions that are present for Jan and slows down the process, taking Jan back to the 'there and then' at the start – away from her 'here and now' concerns. He is working collaboratively with Jan, encouraging her to think and using his distance from the case to enable her to gain an alternative viewpoint on her current anxiety.

THE FUNCTIONS OF SUPERVISION

From the preceding discussion about purpose, it should be clear that supervision has more than one function or task. Wiener et al. (2003, p4) describe four primary tasks of supervision: facilitating, encouraging and informing the work of the supervisee throughout the development of their professional life; attending to the dynamics of the supervisory relationship within an organisational context; ensuring competent and ethical practice is taking place within the developmental stage of the supervisee; and maintaining the good reputation of the profession as a whole – through attention to professional standards and governance.

Within the context of counselling work, Inskipp and Proctor (1993) describe supervision as having *formative*, *normative* (which can be viewed as a monitoring function) and *restorative* qualities. These terms focus on the benefits of supervision for the supervisee. Within the context of social work, Kadushin (1976) offers a broadly similar definition, employing the terms *educative, administrative* (which can be interpreted as managerial) and *supportive*. These terms focus on the role of the supervisor.

Hawkins and Shohet (2006) use the terms *developmental, qualitative* and *resourcing*, and suggest that their definitions add new distinctions to a process that *both supervisor and supervisee are engaged in* (p57). They describe the *developmental* function as being concerned with *developing the skills, understanding and capacity of the supervisees* (p57) via reflection and discussion of client work. Particular stress is placed on the importance of this function, and they state that the collaborative exploration of the work can help the supervisee to:

- *understand the client better;*
- *become more aware of their own reactions and responses to the client;*
- *understand the dynamics of how they and their client were interacting;*
- *look at how they intervened and the consequences of their interventions;*
- *explore other ways of working with this and other similar client situations.*

(Hawkins and Shohet, 2006, p58)

The *qualitative* function of supervision is the monitoring or 'quality control' aspect and helps the practitioner to be mindful of 'human failings', in other words, our blind spots, our own areas of vulnerability and our prejudices and biases. Hawkins and Shohet acknowledge that in many settings the supervisor will also have responsibility for monitoring professional standards, and for ensuring the supervisee is working ethically and appropriately with their client.

The *resourcing* function pays attention to the personal impact of the work on the counsellor. It acknowledges that time is required to express feelings about how the work may affect the supervisee, emotionally and physically. This function of supervision offers resources to counter 'burnout' in a profession where giving of one's self can be burdensome. Practitioners can become *over-identified with their clients or defended against being further affected by them* (Hawkins and Shohet, 2006, p58). This seems very similar to Inskipp and Proctor's restorative function. In explaining the resource function, Hawkins and Shohet make reference to the battle fought by British coal miners in the 1920s against their employers, through which they eventually won the right to *wash off the dirt of their labours* at the pit head in the employer's time – rather than in their own time away from the workplace. *Supervision is the equivalent for those that work at the coal-face of personal distress, disease and fragmentation* (2006, p58).

However, which function is required within a supervisory session at a particular point may not always be clear cut. A presenting issue may appear to be about a formative or developmental task relating to ongoing work with a client, but the restorative or resourcing function may need to be addressed in supervision before the work with a client continues. Ways of working together in supervision will be negotiated through a contract for the work (discussed later in the book), and the focus for the particular session will have been agreed at the start, but, as in work with clients, flexibility is often required. The supervisor testimony that follows illustrates the move from one focus to another.

Case study 1.3 Jaya talking about her supervisory work with Leena, the counsellor

It was a bit of a puzzle for me as Leena is a very experienced counsellor and has counselled young people with a range of issues for many years, and I could not really get to grips with what the barrier was in this particular case. She had said that her client's situation was a little different from her usual experience as he had acquired his dependency following a lengthy illness where drugs were part of his treatment. And we had thought about this and explored it, but Leena said she felt she was not being at all effective. So at the appropriate point we had thought about alternative ways of working with the client and she had said she would reassess the situation and tell me about it next time. I was experiencing some resistance from Leena about trying alternative approaches; this was strange as my sessions with Leena had always felt like we were learning together. I might have challenged her at the time, but decided not to. Well, when we next met it seemed that she had not tried any of the approaches we had discussed, and at that point I wondered what was happening. When I expressed to her the resistance I was feeling, she looked quite shocked. We explored this further, and then she told me about a close family member who had had a similar drug problem following treatment, and she said she had never really spoken about this before. We had assumed that this was an educative task in our supervision, but it turned out there was some restorative work to be done here first. Of course, I listened to what she had to say, but Leena concluded that before she could continue working with her client she needed to address this in her own, personal counselling.

BALANCING THE TASKS OR FUNCTIONS OF SUPERVISION

Alongside the influence of the counselling orientation discussed earlier, the balance of the developmental/formative, qualitative/normative and resourcing/restorative functions may also reflect the preferences of the supervisor according to their role, range of experience and training for the practice of supervision. A supervisor's testimony, building on the response of one of the participants in the study mentioned earlier (Reid, 2010) may help to illustrate this point.

Case study 1.4 Ali

Yeah, we discussed this within the group on the course, you know, the need to balance the functions of formative, normative and restorative. Personally, I feel comfortable with the formative and restorative aspects within supervision, but thinking about it now I guess I pay less attention to the normative function. Of course a lot of the normative or monitoring aspects of the work are covered through training courses and other managerial support. But maybe we need to – I need to – pay more attention to all the functions and not to perhaps assume that the normative function is covered elsewhere. I haven't been in a situation yet where I felt the need to focus much on this function, but I wonder now if subconsciously I avoid this aspect in supervision. In some ways it is a different relationship from what I see as a collaborative role. The normative function is a bit, well, managerial – I'd feel like I was disciplining my supervisee, who is also a colleague. Hmmm, I'll have to think about this some more!

Maintaining the boundaries of expertise within counselling, and supervision, is an ethical practice. From the perspective of the supervisee and in terms of its normative role, supervision has a clear part to play in helping the counsellor to reflect on how they are navigating the (at times) unclear boundaries when working with clients who may require additional counselling or helping services. For novice counsellors this can be particularly important, as the desire to help can lead to interventions that may be beyond their expertise at that stage. Alongside uncomfortable feelings of failure, the practitioner may hide their discomfort rather than discuss the situation within supervision. For Ali, an avoidance of opening up a conversation on such issues meant that, unwittingly, he may be colluding with this behaviour.

The British Association for Counselling in 1988 stated that *the primary purpose of supervision is to ensure that the counsellor is addressing the needs of the client* (p2). This primary definition about the function or purpose of supervision may be an assumption and has been challenged. For example, McMahon and Patton, working with school counsellors, found that:

> *Client welfare received little specific mention by participants . . . support was cited as the predominant benefit of supervision. Many of the participants spoke of support in terms of emotional well-being, the reduction of stress and the prevention of burnout.*

> (2000, p348)

The findings of McMahon and Patton were upheld by this author's study (Reid, 2007a) into the meanings given to supervision by career counsellors who were new to the practice, where, at that time, practitioner self-care was viewed as the primary function. For the practitioners in the study the prime function of supervision was to manage stress and avoid burnout. Of course, stress is not always experienced as a negative force, but time – 'a space' – is required in busy practice to ensure that the high demands of stressful work are matched by adequate supervision (Storey and Billingham, 2001).

In the mental health professions Morrissette (2002) notes that, until relatively recently, very little research attention has been given to the emotional welfare of such helpers. However, the concept of 'burnout', mentioned earlier, has been reviewed extensively in the literature on work organisation and has become a rather over-used term. Morrissette describes the key characteristics of burnout as: extreme dissatisfaction at work; excessive distancing from clients; impaired competence; low energy; increased irritability; depression; and physical, emotional and mental exhaustion. Singularly or together, burnout, performance fatigue, inadequate supervision and the changing context of work (all taking place in an environment that may be target driven and where resources may be insecure) do not facilitate the critical reflection that is viewed as fundamental for effective practice. It would be going too far to suggest that being affected emotionally by the work automatically leads to burnout, but counselling work can be exhausting, and supervision provides a space to process experiences and to continue learning, in order to stay engaged and remain effective. Hawkins and Shohet (2006) note that apathy and loss of interest in the work (as other signifiers of burnout) may be present in counsellors who have stopped learning and are no longer developing at their mid-career point.

But a cautionary note is needed here in terms of emphasising the importance of the restorative function for supervisees. It can lead to practitioners being endlessly self-critical and feeling bound to expose their feelings. If the restorative function is over-used, practitioners are placed in the position where they are sustaining the emotional impact of the work as they must replay the feelings within supervision. This can lead to practitioners breaching the necessary psychological defences they develop in order to contain the emotional impact of the work, and this may counteract the desired professional boundaries between the client and the counsellor.

It is a complex process to keep in balance the focus on the different tasks within supervision, recognise that these tasks often overlap and, at the same time, validate and support the individual. It requires careful thought, preparation, a process and a willingness to learn – by all involved.

It is important to be aware that within the broader counselling literature there is a lack of evidence that demonstrates clearly that supervision directly benefits work with clients if its primary role is viewed as ensuring or safeguarding practice (Lawton and Feltham, 2000). It is a reasonable assumption that it is likely to be beneficial to both counsellors and clients, but, as in the testimony above, there are also aspects of the normative function that can be experienced as surveillance by the supervisee and as policing by the supervisor (Feltham, 2002a; Reid, 2007a). What should be clear by now is that it is the quality of the relationship between the supervisor and supervisee that is crucial in determining its success as a practice to enhance work with clients (Reid and Westergaard, 2006). As in work with clients, the power of being listened to by an attentive practitioner/supervisor should never be underestimated. However, being an experienced and competent counsellor does not automatically mean that the same person is a 'good' supervisor: consider the following testimony.

Case study 1.5 Chris

I have been a counsellor now for six years and feel ready to become a supervisor. During my training I had fantastic supervision and learnt a lot from two different supervisors on separate placements. One was within one-to-one sessions and the other was very skilled at leading group supervision. But I also learnt how not to be a supervisor from two less than great experiences once I qualified. They were both very experienced counsellors. The first supervisor was just so busy, frequently late, preoccupied, kept calling me Christopher – I know it's my name but I had said I prefer Chris and it grates after several sessions! On reflection, I think most of the session was aimed at giving me advice – more efficient for her I suppose. Frankly I don't think she really listened to me – but at least she stayed awake! No really, the other one would nod off occasionally. Anyway what it taught me was how important genuine listening is – the need to attend in very specific ways to my clients. My current supervisor models this well, checks that what we are doing is useful – asks me for feedback and listens to what I say. We work on issues through her posing questions, yeah, and I have learnt so much about my practice – and 'good' supervision!

ACTIVITY 1.2

Make a list of what you think characterises 'good' supervision. The rest of the book should clarify what we think makes it effective and, by extension, 'good', but you might like to review the list you make as you progress through the text.

Before continuing, a cautionary word is required about the assumption that supervision is always a 'good thing' and should therefore be a requirement for counsellors in practice. There is a school of thought that questions this assumption (Feltham, 2002a; Morrissette, 2002), and it is important that this perspective is recognised here. In the USA, for example, supervision is only mandatory for counsellors in training, although many continue to access and receive supervision once fully qualified. There are also significant numbers of practitioners who use counselling skills in their work context in the broader helping professions who do not receive supervision as a matter of course. Recent research (Westergaard, 2012) has highlighted a need for support and supervision for such practitioners. Participants in the research project emphasised the importance of being given an opportunity to reflect on practice in a 'formal' setting, engaging with the qualitative aspect of their work (what they actually do with clients and the impact this has on them) as well as the quantitative element (meeting targets). The activity of supervision was viewed as being central to effective client practice. It could be argued that experienced counsellors should have the opportunity to decide for themselves whether or not traditional supervision methods continue to meet their needs. Currently, however, supervision for counsellors in the UK is mandatory, and even if the choice of opting out was available, research has shown that many counsellors would continue to receive supervision in some form (McMahon and Patton, 2000).

THE GIVING AND RECEIVING OF SUPERVISION

Having looked at the functions of supervision and begun a conversation about what good supervision might look like, it is timely to consider who gives and who receives supervision. An organisation may have the staff capacity to provide 'internal' supervision for trainee, probationary and experienced counsellors, according to the requirements of the relevant professional code of practice. In small organisations or for specialist areas, supervision may be supplied by a supervisor who is external to that agency or group. It is often assumed that supervision is hierarchical, in that a more experienced person supervises the work of a less experienced colleague. However, that may not always be the case, particularly in private practice or voluntary services. There can be difficulties, of course, if supervision is given by an individual's line manager. Dryden et al. (1995) suggest that where a line manager is involved there may be a conflict over the meanings given to supervision, and this can lead to subterfuge on the part of the supervisee. It would be simplistic to say that this can be avoided by keeping supervision outside line management, as capacity issues may restrict the number of supervisors available. In addition, in some contexts it may be the expectation that line managers do give supervision. For example, although organisational goals can take priority, a study by Turner (2000) claimed that many social work practitioners expressed the view that scarce resources ensured that the roles of line manager and supervisor were combined. Separation of the roles was viewed as ideal but unlikely in what was described as an over-stretched service. Research with line managers as supervisors, undertaken by Westergaard (2012), found that the line managers welcomed the supervision aspect of their role.

However, as already discussed, experience and/or seniority does not guarantee effective supervision. Hawkins and Shohet (1989) recommend that if line managers are giving supervision, they should also have a client caseload. This should enable them to have a clear understanding of the situations faced by practitioners, as well as the practice experience to guide supervisees appropriately. We will return to this issue in the final chapter of the book where we discuss the research project mentioned above, which explores line management supervision. In thinking about who gives supervision it will be no surprise to hear that we (Jane and I) believe that there is a requirement for training for the role of supervisor. Holloway and Carroll (1999) also advocate training for supervisors, but we need to question the assumption that formality in the supervision process is always beneficial, and, alongside this, question whether training for supervisors provides a valuable safeguard or a professional constraint. While recognising a need for training, there could be a danger that the formality this brings leads to a teaching approach, rather than facilitating a space for collegiate dialogue in supervision. Training that is based on a singular approach in terms of theory or method may also constrain its applicability in multi-theoretical settings. Above all, as both Weaks (2002) and Wright (2004) conclude, it is the quality of the supervisory relationship that is crucial. In considering the level of experience of a supervisor, Wright asserts: *better a good non-specialist than a less skilled specialist* (2004, p41). So who gives and who receives supervision will be dependent on where the work takes place, the human resources available and the requirements of particular professional contexts.

The other question posed at the start of the chapter was 'Who wants supervision?' In other words, is it for all counsellors all of the time, or are there contested views about this? For many in the UK it will be a requirement in order to practise, but Feltham (2002b) has suggested that in contexts beyond the training stage, some practitioners may practise best without supervision if it is viewed as coercive – a disciplinary practice indicating a lack of trust in their ability to work effectively and professionally. Even if we do not agree with this view and feel that competency is reduced without supervision, it does alert us to the possibility that some counsellors may feel resistant to continuous supervision. As supervisors, we should not assume that all practitioners value the practice all of the time. It is worth noting again in relation to this point that in the USA supervision is not mandatory after the training stage.

A 'SAFE SPACE' FOR EFFECTIVE SUPERVISORY PRACTICE

In Chapter 4 we will discuss one-to-one and group supervision, and introduce other ways of giving and receiving supervision, including creative ways of developing supervisory practice. Chapter 8 will explore creative methodologies more fully, as such alternatives can help to avoid the resistance or lack of interest in continuous supervision that Feltham alerts us to. In addition to the relationship, the theory that underpins the practice and the method used, the effectiveness of supervision will also depend on the location within which supervision take place.

A place away from busy practice to express feelings, doubts, insecurities and discuss 'mistakes' needs to be safe: a contained space. As a term 'busy practice' does not adequately express the effects of work overload, initiative weariness and compassion fatigue. We cannot ignore the issue of resource and time pressures faced by practitioners and their managers, and it might be thought that one time-saving solution would be to offer more group, or peer, supervision opportunities. However, in a large-scale quantitative study Webb and Wheeler (1998) found that counsellors were more able to raise sensitive issues in one-to-one supervision. Conversely, Arkin et al. (1999) discuss the benefits of group supervision in social work and, in particular, its ability to reduce the sense of isolation felt by many practitioners. They state that group supervision can reduce the often hierarchical supervisor/ supervisee relationship and can lead to a clearer conceptualisation of problems related to ethical working and expertise. We should therefore not assume that it is only one-to-one supervision that feels 'safe'.

In thinking about a safe and contained space for 'good' supervision, reference can be made to Winnicott's concept of transitional space (Winnicott, 1971). Winnicott was concerned with what, in early experience, facilitated healthy psychological separation from a prime caregiver and movement towards greater individuation and psychological integration. A 'good enough' mother is one who does not overreact and can contain the child's frustrations and outbursts, but is herself supported by the child's father or another adult: referred to as the 'nursing triad'. In his terms, 'good enough' early relationships provided templates for more fulsome, less anxiety ridden and more playful engagement with experience. 'Good enough' relationships lead to feeling contained and legitimate, as well as valued, in the eyes of significant others. These processes were also seen by Winnicott as foundational for development across a life. Supervision that is 'good enough' is a serious business, but it can also provide an opportunity to play – to engage in and enjoy imaginative and creative learning – providing this takes place in a safe space. Hawkins and Shohet state:

> The supervisor's role is not just to reassure the worker, but to allow the emotional disturbance to be felt within the safer setting of the supervisory relationship, where it can be survived, reflected upon and learnt from. Supervision thus provides a container that holds the helping relationship within the 'therapeutic triad'.
>
> (Hawkins and Shohet, 2006, p3)

Supervision can help the counsellor to develop new approaches alongside 'checking' the boundaries of the work and expressing their frustrations and anxieties. The aim of supervision is for the supervisee to see the problem with greater clarity and, through insight, work towards conclusions about what might be the 'best' solution.

This facilitative approach avoids the danger that the supervisor will view themselves, or be seen by the supervisee, as the expert, there to solve problems and give advice. The type of learning described in this chapter is not about 'teaching the right way of doing things' but about engaging in a dialogue that encompasses the functions of supervision.

CHAPTER SUMMARY

This chapter focused on defining supervision. It discussed:

- the purpose and functions of supervision;
- concepts and issues that will be explored further;
- who receives and who 'gives' supervision;
- what is meant by 'good' supervision;
- the need for a safe space for effective supervision to take place.

SUGGESTED FURTHER READING

Harris, M and Brockbank, A (2011) *An integrative approach to therapy and supervision: a practical guide for counsellors and psychotherapists.* London: Jessica Kingsley Publishers.

As the title suggests, this text draws on ideas from a number of psychological traditions and provides a readable introduction to working with clients and for developing supervisory relationships. Case studies are used to illustrate the use of learning theory for supervision.

Hawkins, P and Shohet, R (2006) *Supervision in the helping professions* (3rd edition). Maidenhead: Open University Press.

This is the third edition of a 'best-selling' text on supervision from well-respected authors. Useful for professionals working within and across different sectors, it is extensive but accessible with examples and case studies. It is a handbook in style, which also incorporates the work and models of other writers – not just the significant contribution of the authors.

CHAPTER 2

The ethical counsellor and supervision

Hazel Reid

CORE KNOWLEDGE

This chapter will provide the opportunity to:

- relate the central importance of ethical behaviour in counselling to supervisory practice;
- examine ethical principles in the context of supervision;
- connect the concepts of multiculturalism and anti-oppressive practice to supervision;
- consider the links between reflexivity and ethical practice;
- explore personal values and their impact on supervisory practice.

INTRODUCTION

Ethical principles, enshrined in standards and codes of practice, underpin counselling, and it is important for the counsellor to reconsider these before entering into a supervisory relationship. Acting ethically is often complex, and professional standards cannot encompass all the ambiguities that are involved in ethical decision making. In counselling, and in supervision, we can be guided by Hippocrates' command that above all else we should 'do no harm', but further guidance is needed. This chapter begins by reviewing ethical principles and relating these to supervisory practice. The chapter moves on to discuss the ethical importance of respecting cultural difference and avoiding oppressive practice. Reflexivity was defined in Chapter 1, and its central role in the development of effective and ethical supervision is examined here. Finally, this chapter helps you to explore, reflexively, your personal values and their potential impact on a supervisory relationship. To begin, the chapter reviews what is meant by 'ethical principles'.

REVIEWING ETHICAL PRINCIPLES

McCulloch (2007, p54) states: *Ethical practice is action that leads to human well-being from a perspective that values the disposition to act truly and justly.* Discussions around ethical principles derive from debates in moral philosophy that took place in the eighteenth and early nineteenth centuries (and, of course, in the ancient world). Leading discourses, or ways of thinking about ethics, define three main perspectives: virtue, consequentialism and deontology. These are reframed by Cribb and Ball (2005) as dispositions, goals and obligations, respectively. There are interesting debates around how the discourses about ethics are shaped, but space limits further discussion here – we will keep the focus on ethics in counselling and supervision. Ethical codes and/or guidelines are developed from a consensual view within counselling, demonstrating that the organisation and its services are accountable. In so doing, they set boundaries around practice. These boundaries aim to protect clients from malpractice, but they can also serve the profession by determining its place within wider 'helping' professions. In other words, such codes also enhance and protect the boundaries around a particular area of expertise (McLeod, 1998), indicating that counsellors must be aware of the limits of their own competence and know when to discuss a referral. When existing codes of practice are found wanting, or professional experience and intuition do not provide a solution, reference can be made to more general ethical principles. The principles of autonomy, non-maleficence, beneficence, justice and fidelity are well known, but are now summarised briefly for this review.

Autonomy refers to the right to freedom of choice and freedom of action, provided that these freedoms do not harm others. In many countries such rights are upheld by legislation. *Non-maleficence* translates as 'above all do no harm'. Even where a client has sought help and given informed consent, the counsellor cannot assume that the responsibility for the consequences of any interaction is that person's alone. *Beneficence* refers to the principle of 'doing good' and promoting human well-being. To fulfil this principle, counsellors ensure they are working within their competence and maintaining and updating their knowledge and skills. *Justice* focuses on the equitable distribution of and access to goods (i.e. resources) and services. Access to those services may, however, be constrained by funding and by policy controls. Finally, *fidelity* relates to the qualities of loyalty, reliability and acting in good faith. Codes relating to confidentiality are informed by the moral and ethical principle of fidelity (and even where there are limits to confidentiality, these limits need to be explicit and explained).

While all of these principles are relevant to counselling, it is possible that they may conflict with each other in some circumstances. Within an increasingly litigious society, adherence to such principles can be difficult and can appear somewhat abstract as they are based upon rational decision making (Banks, 2009). Further, ethical issues cannot be separated from their social and historical context: McLeod states (1998, p274): *Moral concepts such as 'rights' or 'autonomy' only have meaning in relation to the cultural tradition in which they operate.* However, the principles listed above can offer a framework that is useful when considering the ethical dilemmas that arise in the supervision process. Decisions taken in supervision can be related to these ethical principles. Documenting the discussion that leads to a particular decision is helpful to justify the approach taken and, consequently, can also protect those involved, should evidence to support the decision be required in any subsequent complaint (Scaife, 2001). But while there is common ground from which a consensus results, there will be times when the supervisor or the supervisee face ethical problems and ethical dilemmas – we will return to this shortly.

RELATING ETHICAL PRINCIPLES TO SUPERVISION

We have now reviewed general ethical principles – but how do they relate to the practice of supervision? At this point, extensive reference could be made to relevant ethical codes (e.g. BACP, 2010) and, of course, you will want to be familiar with your own professional organisation's latest code of practice and ethics for supervision. However, before moving on it may be more interesting to start with a 'blank page' and think about the ethical principles that you would like to be evident in a supervisory relationship.

REFLECTION POINT

What would be most important for you? What would you wish to be evident in supervisory work, enacted by both the supervisor and the supervisee?

Hawkins and Shohet (2006, p54–55) propose six basic principles for supervision.

1. Balancing appropriate responsibility for the work of the supervisee with respect for their autonomy.
2. Due concern for the well-being and protection of the client with respect for their autonomy.
3. Acting within the limits of one's own competence and knowing when to seek further help.
4. Fidelity – being faithful to explicit and implicit promises made.
5. Anti-oppressive practice.
6. Openness to challenge and feedback combined with an active commitment to ongoing learning.

WHEN ETHICAL PRINCIPLES CONFLICT

Life is complicated, and it is not possible to approach ethical decision making purely from an objective stance. For example, I might decide on what is the best action for my client, based on the principle of beneficence, but my decision may conflict with my client's wishes. If I proceeded without taking into consideration my client's views, I would be disregarding the principle of autonomy – of the client. My approach would need to consider the client's right to choose, alongside taking account of who has the right to judge what is 'for the good'.

The counsellor and the supervisor will often face ethical problems and ethical dilemmas that occur when principles are in conflict. Solutions can often be found for problems, but – by definition – ethical dilemmas are more difficult to solve, and turning to ethical codes and general principles may not provide an answer. What follows are a number of case studies that demonstrate how principles can conflict within supervision. For each, you might add an activity by asking yourself: *Hmm, what would I do in these circumstances?*

Case study 2.1 Jane and Jo

Jane is worried about her supervisee Jo, who appears to be very anxious. Jo starts the session by talking about what is going on in her personal life. The more she talks the more agitated she becomes, and Jane is concerned that neither of them will be able to contain the anxiety within the supervision session. Jo then reveals that when life became unbearable in the past she attempted suicide. Jane is concerned about what will happen when Jo leaves. Will she be safe?

ACTIVITY 2.1

What ethical principles apply here? How do they influence the next step and what action should be taken? What would *you* do in these circumstances?

You would want to act in good faith (*fidelity*) as it is likely that Jo has made her revelation expecting it to be confidential. But you would also want to 'do the right thing' (*beneficence*), and that need is likely to conflict with respecting Jo's *autonomy*. If you were working with a young or vulnerable client, your agreed contract is likely to have covered the issue of confidentiality and what is to happen if this needs to be overruled to prevent self-harm or harm to others. In a supervisory relationship, intervening because you are worried about Jo's mental health and safety might conflict with your supervisory contract. But you would also be thinking about the principle of *non-maleficence* if your supervisee is currently working with clients. You would want to protect your supervisory contract with Jo, but the issue may be one for counselling for Jo, rather than supervision. Containing Jo's anxiety would be important within the session, and listening to what she has to say is essential, but this is unlikely to be enough. A prompt referral might be the next best step if Jo agrees, but can you insist? The nature of supervision is such that Jane cannot 'un-know' what she has been told. She may feel she now has vicarious responsibility for Jo. It is crucial that the decision taken is shared and documented, framed against the ethical principles discussed.

Case study 2.2 Janna and Paul

Janna has worked as a supervisor with Paul, a trainee counsellor, over several sessions. Paul loves his supervision sessions and is very keen to learn. He contacts Janna by email regularly to check out issues he is facing in practice. Janna is beginning to feel a bit worn out by the attention and enthusiasm, but more importantly she is concerned that Paul just does not seem to 'get it', despite the hours of input. Janna likes Paul and wants to support his development, but is concerned about his apparent lack of ability to take responsibility for his own learning and progress.

ACTIVITY 2.2

What ethical principles apply here? How do they influence the next step and what action should be taken? What would you do in these circumstances?

As the supervisor you would be concerned about Paul's clients if Paul is not learning (*non-maleficence*), but you want to treat Paul fairly and give him every opportunity to learn (*justice*). Alongside this you would need to think about your own well-being, as Paul's demands are becoming excessive. The final decision is likely to be influenced by what is best for Paul's clients. You would want to give Paul enough time to become an independent learner before you wonder if he is perhaps not suited to the occupation and needs career counselling.

Case study 2.3 Leroy and Jaycee

Leroy enjoys his supervision meetings with Jaycee, but begins to reflect on this. He becomes aware that there is a sexual attraction between himself and his supervisee, and his feeling is that this is mutual. He wonders if it is getting in the way of the functions of supervision and thinks it is his responsibility to do something about this.

ACTIVITY 2.3

What ethical principles apply here? How do they influence the next step and what action should be taken? What would you do in these circumstances?

It might be thought that counsellors and supervisors in their adherence to the principle 'above all else do no harm', might be 'above' such behaviour – but counsellors and supervisors are human beings, of course, and sexual attraction may be more prevalent than we think. In Case study 2.3 any sexual advance on the part of Leroy might be coercive and would act against upholding Jaycee's *autonomy*, even if the attraction is mutual. It is unlikely in such circumstances that the supervisory contract would be maintained. Leroy should seek advice, which is likely to be that the supervisory relationship must end. He will then be in the difficult position of having to explain to his supervisee why the contract has been terminated. However, when we consider both the supervisee and the potential effects on the supervisee's work, it could be argued that all the ethical principles apply in this case. Using immediacy and being congruent with his supervisee would be important when he explains why the supervision must end.

Case study 2.4 Maria and Danna

Maria has begun working with a new supervisee, Danna, a qualified counsellor, who states she will report verbally rather than share recordings of her counselling sessions. Maria's expectation was that they would discuss case studies through observation of work – either live or recorded – as that is the norm within the counselling organisation. However, Maria has never liked this approach herself when it comes to her own work, so she agrees to Danna's declaration. Once sessions begin, she has second thoughts and realises she has colluded with Danna to avoid a difficulty that is as much hers as her supervisee's.

ACTIVITY 2.4

What ethical principles apply here? How do they influence the next step and what action should be taken? What would you do in these circumstances?

On one level we would want to uphold the supervisee's *autonomy* and her right to choose the approach to supervision. This would be an issue with a supervisee who was in training as the work needs to be observed before qualifying, but Danna is at the post-registration stage. What might be important here – if observation is the norm within the organisation – is to explore why Danna does not want her work observed. Maria also needs to consider her own developmental needs and not hide from them, using Danna's difficulty to cover up her own unease at being observed. Unless this is addressed, the work of both supervisor and supervisee may violate the principles of *justice, beneficence* and *non-maleficence* as fewer safeguards are in place when compared to other counsellors within their organisation.

LEGAL REQUIREMENTS

Decision making in supervision will also be informed by legal requirements, and these will be bound by the working context, professional codes and the law within a particular country or state. As with work with clients, when in doubt a supervisor should examine codes of conduct, seek advice and document their action. Underpinning the need to be aware of legal requirements is the fear of litigation. When working with children, for example, making a mistake can have very serious consequences. Following the Gillick ruling (*Gillick* v *Norfolk and Wisbech AHA*, 1985) the law in England and Wales allows practitioners working with children to provide a confidential service. Mrs Gillick requested that her local health authority should not be allowed to give contraceptive advice to her daughters, who were under sixteen years of age. The eventual judgement revolved around whether children under the age of sixteen were competent to make decisions regarding their own medical treatment. The ruling stated that a child is considered to be competent according to chronological age alongside mental and emotional maturity, intelligence and comprehension of the issue: this is known as Gillick competence. The Gillick ruling can be applied outside medical situations, and therefore includes confidentiality in counselling, but it can be overturned in cases where a child may be refusing help in a life and death situation. What might be contentious here is the duty of mandatory reporting, but the Gillick ruling still applies, despite more recent events – for example, following the Laming Inquiry into the death of Victoria Climbié (DoH, 2003). While the Gillick ruling relates to preserving the confidentiality of the client, the best place to discuss difficult issues will be in supervision. The supervisor can help the supervisee to examine the ethics, balancing protection for vulnerable clients within the framework of the counselling process and the organisation's code of conduct or legal requirements. Action may need to be immediate, but the resulting anxiety can be contained within supervision.

There are other ethical and legal issues that may arise in supervision. Examples are: whether there is a 'duty to warn' in the case of the possibility of a serious crime; engaging in fair and due process if a supervisee's competence to practise is a concern; and becoming party to information about a supervisee's colleague who, the supervisor is told, is engaging in misconduct and actions that are discriminatory.

CULTURAL 'DIFFERENCE' AND ANTI-OPPRESSIVE PRACTICE

Counsellors should be aware that they operate from cultural assumptions that need to be questioned. Scaife draws on a broad definition of culture, stating:

> Differences between people along the dimensions of ethnicity, culture, gender, sexual orientation, age and disability have provided a context for discrimination in favour of the dominant group throughout our cultural history. Ethical practice under the principle of justice requires an equitable approach be made to different groups whether these involve clients and/or supervisees.
>
> (Scaife, 2001, p134)

Deeply held values and beliefs arising from culture – in its widest terms – can have a negative impact on the practice of supervision. The term anti-oppressive practice helps us to think of this as an approach that is not limited to race or ethnicity – as in the quote from Scaife above. As a first step towards anti-oppressive practice, cultural 'difference' on both sides of the supervisory relationship should be explored from the start of the relationship. This exploration can help to address any 'blind spots' or assumptions that may be influencing the work. Bimrose (2006, p74) suggests that an acknowledgement of difference *is important at various levels. For example (and perhaps most obviously), it is important for the critical review of practice that is at the heart of this activity [supervision].* As Bimrose goes on to explain, this is particularly relevant where there is difference in terms of power and status, both within an organisation and within the dominant culture. A case can be made for matching supervisor and supervisee – for example, a black supervisor with a black supervisee. The intention would be to acknowledge that there may be experiences in common based on membership of a minority group. However, this can be founded on a false assumption that both parties belong to the same cultural group, and it is itself a kind of tyranny. Scaife supports this point: *Even the act to decide to consult with the supervisee about her or his preference prior to making the allocation singles the person out if this is not the usual procedure* (2001, p139). A case study will illustrate this point.

Case study 2.5 Margaret

Margaret was born and educated in South East Asia and has recently moved to the UK to join the rest of her family. She has now qualified, having undertaken her counselling qualification at a large university based in a multi-ethnic city. An opportunity arose for a job as a counsellor in a town on the south coast of England, and Margaret was delighted when she was offered the position – which she accepted. She works mainly with adults in a small counselling service. When she met the line manager for the first time, the question of organising appropriate supervision was raised. Seeing that Margaret had her head covered, he said: *I'm not sure what to do about your supervision as we do not have any other counsellors who are Muslim within our small group.* Margaret did not know how to reply as she was not expecting different treatment from any of her new colleagues. She felt, she said, *flattened* by this statement and *as if I was a bit of a nuisance.* On reflection, she thought he was probably trying to be culturally sensitive, but she felt his concern was both insensitive and misplaced.

A better approach from the line manager would have been to avoid making assumptions and ask Margaret about her expectations and preferences regarding supervision, outlining the limitations that existed within a small organisation for any counsellor – regardless of ethnicity, culture, gender or age. The approach taken by the line manager is oppressive rather than anti-oppressive (Thompson, 1993). What was required was the development of multicultural competence – essential in counselling and relevant also for supervision. Multicultural competence is discussed in detail in Reid (2011), and readers are directed there for further information. But, drawing on that publication, principled action that works towards multicultural competence in supervision can be informed by the matrix (as outlined in Reid, 2011) offered by Sue et al. (1995) for counselling. Points can include:

- awareness of own biases and limitations and their outcomes;
- recognition of the range of social variables that lead to cultural difference;
- knowledge about the causes and effects of oppression, racism, discrimination and stereotyping;
- openness about processes of supervision with a view to a collaborative approach that works alongside the supervisee;

- commitment to enriching understanding through continuous professional and reflexive development;
- searching for appropriate and culturally sensitive models of supervision, rather than reliance on established or 'singular' methods;
- awareness and understanding of the impact of negative treatment experienced by marginalised groups;
- respect for people's beliefs, values and views about themselves and the stories they choose to tell the supervisor;
- valuing the language, style and manner of speech, while acknowledging there will be times when the supervisor's linguistic skills will be inadequate;
- questioning of the appropriateness and helpfulness of organisational supervision methods;
- awareness of institutional practices that lead to discrimination;
- congruence when considering how to overcome relevant discrimination;
- understanding of the differences in communication styles and their impact, plus extension of own communication skills and methods;
- open-mindedness to alternative ways of supporting, including using the resources of the supervisee.

As should be obvious, the first step in developing this competence is self-awareness, exploring the bias that underpins our assumptions about ourselves and others, and the Western discourses that underpin counselling theory and practice. It is important to stress again that 'difference' is not just related to race or ethnicity, although often it is the most visible difference and the historical circumstances that lead to racial discrimination should never be underplayed. An exploration of personal values is provided in the final activity in this chapter, but the need for self-awareness brings us back to the importance of reflexivity in supervision.

REFLEXIVITY IN SUPERVISION

In the previous chapter definitions of reflectivity and reflexivity were offered. They are worth repeating here before we continue. A reflective practitioner is someone who is able to reach potential solutions through analysing experience and prior knowledge, in order to inform current and future practice. The internal process of reflection that is active and conscious could be described as reflectivity. Reflexivity is the process by which we are aware of our own responses to what is happening in a particular context (i.e. a counselling interaction or supervision session) and our reactions to people, events and the dialogue taking place. A reflexive understanding will include an awareness of the personal, social and cultural context and its influence on both the speaker and the listener. Reflexive awareness in counselling practice leads to a deeper understanding of how we co-construct knowledge about the world, and ways of operating within it, that are more meaningful for those involved.

If we view supervision as a learning process, it would be reasonable to suggest that contemporary learning theories promote the concept of reflection as a route to so-called 'deep' learning (Brockbank and McGill, 2007). Deep learning through reflexive processes should lead to cognitive learning: i.e. changes in our understanding of the world, and in ways of behaving in the world. Such learning takes place in a social context with others and is affected by the degree of agency (or personal power and influence) that the learner possesses or can access (Harris and Brockbank, 2011). How supervision is structured, the models and methods employed, the cultural conditions within which it is 'delivered' and the type of organisation within which it is set will all affect the learning process. The space for learning is also created, and often constrained by, the language used – the ways of speaking and thinking in a particular context (referred to earlier as discourses). The prevailing discourse will draw on a particular set of meanings, a shared understanding of the use of metaphors, images that have resonance within a particular setting and cultural stories that are meaningful to the particular group (Burr, 1995). The understanding involved is often assumed and, as a prevailing discourse, is given precedence over other ways of talking and thinking – in other words, of representing the world. In order to belong to a particular group, such discourses have to be understood and joined with. Clearly, some discourses are more powerful than others, and the space for resisting the prevailing discourse may be highly constrained. Such matters affect a person's capacity to learn and are influential in supervision. A case study may help to illustrate the point.

Case study 2.6 Jenny meets Miranda, her new supervisor

Jenny works in an inner city area with young people who present with a range of issues that are often connected to the disadvantages associated with the area, e.g. unemployment, poor housing, underfunded schooling and what the media describe as 'rival gang culture'. She qualified as a counsellor two years ago and enjoys her work, although it is often very challenging. She is the only counsellor working within a charitable organisation with young people from a particular large housing estate. Although she works 'safely', she often feels isolated and values her supervision sessions. She felt a bit bereft when Pat told her she was retiring and would no longer be her supervisor, but she is relieved to hear that the organisation has arranged for her to have supervision elsewhere. An appointment is made to meet Miranda, her new supervisor.

After the meeting Jenny tells her partner what happened: *It was a nice building, easy to find, but I felt a bit anxious when I arrived, and the first impression of Miranda was, blimey, she just oozes upper class! She was friendly, shook my hand, offered me*

---

tea and after the usual introductions invited me to talk about my work, education and training. Well, I didn't say much as I doubted she'd be impressed with my university and I doubt she works with kids like mine! She then told me a little about her own story, where she went after university – Oxbridge, I suspect, although she did not name the place. She was trying really hard, but I just didn't feel comfortable. She was a bit, well, la-di-da! And she clearly had difficulty with my accent. I dunno, it was as difficult for her as it was for me I guess. At one point she was saying something about reflexive practice and making some reference to a character in a book that I don't know about – hadn't got a clue what she meant, but I didn't want to let on that I didn't understand. I then just spent most of the time feeling a bit stupid and miserable, missing Pat. We are not well matched, she lives in a different world to me, but how can I say I want someone else? I work for a charity after all, and she is far more experienced than me! I don't know what to do about this – what do you think?

In the case study above, Jenny does not feel as if she has much agency in terms of the choice of supervisor, and unless the relationship develops positively, it seems doubtful at this stage that her capacity to learn will be met. Jenny is reflecting on the meeting, but as yet she does not know what, if anything, she can do about the situation.

REFLECTION POINT

If you were Jenny's partner, how would you respond?

The literature on reflective practice for learning within supervision is helpful here. Specifically, Harris and Brockbank (2011) draw on the work of Argyris and Schön (1996) and Hawkins and Shohet (1989), and the discussion of single and double loop learning within supervision. In the case study, Jenny is reflecting on what happened, thinking about the relationship and wanting to find a solution. She is at the start of a process of single loop reflection and learning that is well known and associated with Kolb (1984). If Jenny engages in further *reflection* on what took place, she may decide to *revise* her behaviour at the next meeting by being more assertive, making sure she questions metaphors or language she does not understand. Through *testing* this revised approach she will gain a new *experience*, and she can reflect on the results. If all goes well, she will gain confidence in her ability and will have learnt about herself and how to change this supervisory relationship in the process.

For transformative learning to take place, a deeper change is required. Harris and Brockbank state: *really effective learning is characterised by the transition from single to double loop learning which enables the learner to move beyond their existing way of working with the support and challenge, using reflective dialogue, of their therapist or supervisor* (2011, pp55–56).

To engage in double loop learning Jenny needs to consider if her own beliefs and/or assumptions are influencing her approach to her supervisor and then move to take a new stance by looking at the situation from a different perspective. To do this she needs to shift her ways of thinking about the world and open up a space for the new learning and understanding that arises from this – and the way to achieve this is through reflexive dialogue with her supervisor.

Case study 2.7 Jenny talks about the next meeting

Yeah, it was much better, thanks. I thought about what you said and decided I would ask if I did not understand, but actually I went back to some of my notes about reflexive behaviour from the course. At the time it obviously didn't sink in, but rereading these I realised I was making some assumptions about Miranda and not really thinking about my behaviour in that first meeting. I hadn't really thought about this specifically in terms of supervision – and of course Pat, my previous supervisor, well, her background was very similar to mine. Anyway I started to question why I felt so negatively about Miranda, when she was friendly, welcoming, wanted to get to know me and was interested in my work. It's not easy to say this, but my negative view was down to my background, not hers. She was good, though, as she had obviously picked up on this last time, but didn't want to push it early on in our work together. She said that she got the sense that I was feeling uncomfortable that first time and asked me if I could describe my emotions after I left. Well, that got me energised, but I managed to do this in an open way and she thanked me. Turns out she didn't go to Oxbridge, and she's done a lot of work in family therapy in some pretty difficult places here in the UK and abroad.

Her approach in the session was very, I don't know, connected – it was me that had been judgemental. She said at one point – about a case we began to discuss – that it was a situation she had not experienced and she wanted me to help her understand it. What really struck me afterwards, thinking about that first visit, is that I'm not like that with clients – like, judgemental. I really try to get to know them on their terms, and that was what Miranda was working towards with me. Anyway we had an interesting 'dialogue', to use Miranda's term, and it felt collaborative. Yeah, I left feeling stimulated and wished we could have had a longer session. Still, there's next time.

Jenny's final insight in the case study is important. It is often much easier to see and understand the behaviour of others than it is to see and understand our own. To do so and act upon our discoveries requires a high level of reflexivity, and supervision can provide the space to nurture such reflexive behaviour: leading to transformative learning and change. One other aspect in Jenny's case study that is worth further thought is the place that emotion plays in transformative learning. Jenny's crisis involved her emotions, i.e. she felt stupid and miserable, and was missing Pat. She was not suppressing those emotions, however, and wanted to address the problem. Mezirow (1994, p223) tells us that for a shift in our understanding to occur, so that meaning can be transformed, we need to engage in a process where we critique our assumptions by *examining their origins, nature and consequences*. Strong emotion can also include expressing positive feelings that describe the learning: Jenny now says she left feeling stimulated and wanting more. With Miranda's support she is constructing a collaborative space for learning within supervision.

PERSONAL VALUES AND SUPERVISION

Within the helping professions, ethical and moral issues cannot be separated from questions relating to values. A value can be defined as a lasting and firm belief that a particular style of conduct is preferable to any other. Values are shaped by historical and cultural settings and, in professional contexts, by the particular social and theoretical developments within the field. Assumptions that such values are shared must be questioned, and the ethical practitioner will, as has been said above, want to explore the background of their own value position in order to achieve anti-oppressive practice (Thompson, 1993).

The helping professions, including counselling, draw significantly on the discipline of psychology and have their roots in values that assume that the individual has it within their power to change for the better – 'better' here meaning what the mainstream society defines as socially acceptable behaviour. This individualistic view, which has dominated the traditional approaches within psychology, ignores how an individual's 'success' is shaped by the social, cultural, historical and political context within which they operate (Parker, 2007).

Ethics, based on values that are underpinned by the discipline of psychology alone, can be problematic if issues related to power and position are not considered. However, while it is important to recognise the influence of such complex issues, problems in practice are rarely addressed if action is always viewed as, ultimately, ineffective.

ACTIVITY 2.5

Consider what influences your personal values and how those influences might affect your approach to supervision – as a supervisee or a supervisor.

One way of approaching this is to think about your name, your place of birth, your background and your cultural history. What story would you tell about yourself? Make brief notes on that story.

Think about the discussion in this chapter. How might your biography influence your values within supervision?

Much of what has been covered in this chapter resonates with ethical issues in counselling practice. Attention to these issues forms a sound bedrock for considering ethical issues in supervision. When an ethical dilemma occurs, Corey et al. (1993) suggest the following as a step-by-step process to work towards ethically sound decisions, recommending that each stage should be documented.

- Identify the problem or dilemma.
- Identify the potential issues involved.
- Review relevant ethical guidelines.
- Discuss and consult with a colleague.
- Consider possible and probable courses of action.
- Enumerate the possible consequences of various decisions.
- Decide what appears to be the best course of action.

(cited in Scaife, 2001, p144)

Of course, as in counselling practice, things happen in the moment, and there is often a desire to act immediately. In many cases it will be appropriate to wait and use the phrase *I'll need to think about that some more and get back to you*, but additional advice would be to make sure you do so and in a timely fashion.

So, at a practical level, ethical codes do attempt to address ethical problems and to regulate professional behaviour. They exist to protect the service user (the client) and the practitioner in a society that requires agencies (and their professionals) to be accountable for the services offered. Codes are more than guidelines – guidelines appear optional whereas a 'code' implies a system of laws to be followed, based on a prevailing standard of agreed moral behaviour. Codes serve to unify a group of people around a common purpose and, by so doing, help to define that purpose. Professional codes of conduct within the helping services are usually, but not exclusively (Daniels and Jenkins, 2010), governed by the legislative framework within a particular country.

Responsible and reflexive practice requires a practitioner to interpret (rather than just follow) the codes of practice that govern their work and to develop an attitude of *ethical watchfulness* (Reid, 2004). At the heart of ethical watchfulness, however, lies a respect for persons and an acknowledgement of the defining principles discussed at the start of this chapter: autonomy, non-maleficence, beneficence, justice and fidelity.

CHAPTER SUMMARY

This chapter focused on ethical practice in supervision. It explored:

- general ethical principles found in counselling;
- ethical principles in the context of supervision;
- concepts of multiculturalism and anti-oppressive practice;
- the links between reflexivity, ethical practice and supervision;
- personal values and their impact on supervisory practice.

SUGGESTED FURTHER READING

Bimrose, J (2006) Multicultural issues in support and supervision, in Reid, HL and Westergaard, J (eds) *Providing support and supervision: an introduction for professionals working with young people.* Abingdon: Routledge.

The issues regarding supervision and the broad concept of multiculturalism are discussed in depth in this chapter. Although the book relates to work with young people, the issues explored are not confined to age.

Bond, T (2010) *Standards and ethics for counselling in action,* 3rd edition. London: Sage.

Daniels, D and Jenkins, P (2010) *Therapy with children: children's rights, confidentiality and the law,* 2nd edition. London: Sage.

For a thorough understanding of the ethical, contractual and legal requirements of counselling, these two books are very useful.

Scaife, J (2001) *Supervision in the mental health professions: a practitioner's guide.* Hove: Brunner/Routledge.

This is a comprehensive text on supervision written in an accessible style – the chapter on ethics is particularly helpful.

CHAPTER 3

Theoretical frameworks for supervision

Hazel Reid

CORE KNOWLEDGE

This chapter will provide the opportunity to:

- consider a number of theoretical models developed for supervisory practice;
- examine concepts from psychodynamic therapy;
- explore the drama triangle in supervision;
- locate your individual perspective.

INTRODUCTION

So far we have considered the purpose and the functions of supervision, and the importance of reflexive, ethical and multicultural practice. In this chapter we explore theoretical frameworks that can be used to structure supervision. Hawkins and Shohet (2006, p56) use the expression *maps and models* to describe the various theories, types and styles that can inform an approach to supervision that 'matches' the supervisee and the context within which they work. Wiener et al. (2003) highlight how different authors draw on various concepts and theories to explain and situate the purpose and functions of supervision.

As indicated by the references in this book, many authors have highlighted the need for providing 'tools to think with' – theories – that are developed specifically for supervision, rather than assuming that a qualified counsellor can 'do' supervision because they are counsellors. Supervisors navigate different waters, and the knowledge gained from counselling practice will be helpful, but it may not provide an adequate understanding of the meanings present in supervision. At the same time, we need to be aware of the dangers of over-structuring supervision in what is a relational activity – subjective and emotional.

With those reservations in mind, the focus of this chapter is to introduce those new to supervision to a number of maps and models that can frame supervisory practice. There are others that cannot be included, and at the end of the chapter further reading is suggested. Many of the models that are introduced here will be elaborated in later chapters, when the book moves on to describe the preparation, establishment, development, maintenance and ending of the supervisory relationship. This chapter also explores ideas from Gestalt and psychodynamic therapy that inform supervision, before looking at how the drama triangle might be enacted within the supervisory relationship. Finally, you are invited to consider your own position and locate your theoretical perspective, or perspectives, with regard to the maps and models that are likely to be appropriate for you.

STRUCTURING A SUPERVISORY RELATIONSHIP

Chapters 5 and 6 of this book detail the processes involved in beginning a supervisory relationship – in many ways, these mirror the start of a counselling relationship. Simply put, thought is given to the supervision process before it begins, and to the contract negotiated to work towards a shared agenda. Confidentiality and its limits are discussed, as the supervisor has a duty to the profession, the organisation, the supervisee and the counselling client. The way in which the supervisor and supervisee work towards a working alliance is discussed, alongside a discussion of strategies and actions for achieving those goals. For all this to happen, a structure is required, and the process for structuring supervision is likely to resonate with the theoretical perspective of the counselling approach, albeit the approach needs to be relevant to particular contexts.

Explanatory models grounded in counselling and psychotherapeutic practice can be applied to supervision. To begin, we will consider the model derived from developmental theory described by Stoltenberg and Delworth (1987), followed by the seven-eyed model of Hawkins and Shohet (2006). These two models are well known and provide a useful starting point for this introductory text. Following this, we will look in brief at how ideas from cognitive behavioural therapy, solution focused work and narrative counselling can be related to supervision, before outlining integrative approaches.

A DEVELOPMENTAL MODEL

Stoltenberg and Delworth's model focuses on the developmental stage of the counsellor and helps the supervisor and supervisee to understand the dynamics at work within the supervisory relationship. The discussion of this should be open, to deepen reflexivity within the developmental process. The model presents a four-level process of professional development, as follows.

- *Level one: self-centred* The supervisee is likely to have a high level of dependence on their supervisor. They may be feeling anxious about their work and be relatively inexperienced, unable to engage in informed reflection. Their view of self-competence may not be positive.

- *Level two: people centred* The supervisee fluctuates between feeling secure in their work and feeling unsure and, at times, overwhelmed by its complexities. They can be at one time very enthusiastic and at others defensive.

- *Level three: process centred* The development reaches a stage where the supervisee has increased their level of professional security and is less dependent on the supervisor. Equality is being achieved in the relationship, and greater time is spent on the process of the work, in a more holistic manner.

- *Level four: process in context* The professional development of the supervisee at this level could be described as autonomous. The level of skills is high. The supervisee will be demonstrating self-awareness, insight and a developed level of reflection in relation to a wide range of features within the work.

The role of the supervisor when applying Stoltenberg and Delworth's model is to consider which level their supervisee is working at and to support them to move on – develop – to the next stage. Stoltenberg et al. (1998) refined the model into an integrated development model (IDM), which incorporates the four levels identified above into three stages of development. Much more is said about applying the IDM in Chapter 7, but a pause for reflection on the four levels described above would be useful here.

REFLECTION POINT

Reflecting on the four levels, where would you place your own development in terms of supervision – as a supervisee? Why? This will probably depend on your level of experience as a counsellor.

A PROCESS MODEL

The seven-eyed model of Hawkins and Shohet (2006) has as its focus the supervision process rather than the supervisee's development. The seven key areas (or eyes with which to observe the work) are:

1. the client;
2. the intervention;

3. the relationship;
4. the supervisee;
5. the parallel process;
6. the supervisor;
7. the socio-cultural context.

Within the model, a balance needs to be struck in terms of the time spent exploring each of these aspects. So, for example, it would be appropriate to look at the counselling context by describing (1) the client's history, circumstances and the evaluation of the 'case', but supervision needs to focus on the practitioner too – their practice. The work should move on to consider (2) the intervention. What work has been completed so far? Together, supervisor and supervisee can examine the actual practice and assess its effectiveness. This can lead to discussing alternative techniques and ways of implementing these. It will also be important to explore (3) the relationship with the client. How does it feel to be working with this person? Are there difficulties that need to be examined? A focus on this aspect will provide space for the supervisee to reflect on the quality of the relationship with their client and consider how this could be changed, as appropriate.

The restorative function of supervision can be enhanced by time spent talking about the supervisee's views about themselves in this work (4). How do they feel and think about their counselling practice? How does this relate to 'their story', both personally and professionally? How do they feel about the supervisory relationship? This focus provides an opening to discuss and process some of the difficulties in the work, but also to celebrate success. The parallel process (5) is described in more detail later in the chapter, but briefly, attention is paid to what is happening in the supervisory relationship that can provide insight into the work with a client. And as supervision is a relationship, the supervisor (6) will be thinking about their supervisory practice as a result of the dialogical process. How does the supervisor feel about the supervisory work? Are they able to 'park' their own work, and other roles they may have if working in the same organisation, and focus on the needs of the supervisee? The final aspect to consider is the socio-cultural context (7). Counselling takes place within wider organisational, social and cultural contexts, and this wider setting needs to be considered. At times the impact will be obvious – for example, if the client has engaged in illegal activity that has consequences for the counselling relationship, or if services or the level of resources have changed. At other times the impact may be less obvious and may relate to the cultural background of those involved. Application of the seven-eyed model is also developed in Chapter 7, which focuses on progressing the supervisory relationship. If you would like further explanation now, you could look at the case studies in Chapter 7.

COGNITIVE BEHAVIOURAL, SOLUTION-FOCUSED AND NARRATIVE APPROACHES TO SUPERVISION

In any introductory text it is always difficult to know where to 'draw the line' between what someone new to supervision would like to explore and all that is available to examine. Whole books could be written on any theoretical framework for supervision, and I am hesitant to reduce to a few paragraphs the explanations of the ones listed in the heading. With that in mind, I will avoid peppering the short descriptions that follow with references – but the reader unfamiliar with these approaches will want to consult the sources referred to in the suggested texts at the end of the chapter. So, apologies aside, in order to excite an interest in the reader to find out more the aim here is to signpost a range of theoretical approaches in counselling and psychotherapy that can be applied to supervision.

Cognitive behavioural approaches and supervision

Cognitive behavioural therapy (CBT) has as its focus the learning of new skills and behaviours to alter or end behaviour that is problematic or damaging in some way. It would not be correct to say that feelings are ignored, but there is less of a focus on feelings. Traditionally, the mechanistic view of effecting change was more akin to teaching for enabling positive skills – as behaviour is learned it can be 'unlearned'. That said, current CBT practitioners do recognise and place importance on the relationship within counselling and recognise that this is an important aspect in working towards change. The emphasis in CBT is on specific issues and thought patterns, where clients are directed towards their negative self-talk and self-defeating beliefs. The aim is to work towards behaviour that counters this, to develop more positive beliefs about the self and to act from this more balanced position. In supervision, the supervisor can use knowledge of CBT to help the supervisee to identify any patterns in the work with their client. Such patterns may be influenced by a lack of awareness of the supervisee's own thoughts and behaviours toward the client and the work with the client. As CBT has an emphasis on skills, the supervisor can discuss techniques that may be useful and give the supervisee an opportunity to practise these – in the session or outside the session as a 'homework' task. They can then evaluate the technique together. A case study follows to illustrate this brief introduction.

Case study 3.1 I find it difficult to say *Time's up*

Janine is a qualified counsellor who tells her supervisor that she is finding work with her client, Gloria, difficult. She feels rather overwhelmed by Gloria, who constantly interrupts her, often arrives late and then is unwilling to leave when the session should come to an end. Janine has tried to make it clear that late arrival will shorten the session, but Gloria always has some 'reasonable' excuse. Janine and her supervisor agree that role playing some assertiveness techniques would be useful. Before trying this in the session, they have a discussion about the differences between aggressive, passive and assertive behaviour. To engage in the role play of assertive counsellor and the client, Gloria, the supervisor and supervisee swap roles at times to try out the new responses from both sides. In this way Janine gets an opportunity to build her confidence through learning this new behaviour. At the next supervision session she will feedback how this worked in counselling with Gloria.

Solution-focused approaches and supervision

Counsellors working from the solution-focused approach do not assume that is it is necessary to explore a problem in depth or to analyse its causes in order to help clients to progress. Solution-focused work pays attention to solution building and what *is* working in terms of moving towards and achieving desired outcomes. Solution-focused work departs from earlier 'positivist' or scientific approaches in counselling and therapy by recognising that perspectives on 'reality' are constructed by individuals in relationships with others. Supervision, like counselling, is an interactive process, and techniques that are used in solution-focused counselling can be applied to supervision. Thus, in a similar way, the main aim in supervision is maintaining a focus on the intended results of the work and using this as a means to structure supervision. Through collaboration the focus should be specific and the supervisee should leave a session with a clear idea about the direction of the work and steps to be taken.

Core concepts from solution-focused counselling include assuming that change is inevitable and that interventions will build upon the individual's strengths. This is seen as furthering motivation, to enhance a belief that change is possible. There is an avoidance of problem-saturated stories – albeit that the issue needs to be clarified – as the focus is on finding solutions. The supervisor's role is not that of expert, but of facilitator. Concepts from solution-focused counselling that can be used for supervision include:

- searching for the detail in the story told;
- considering what works now and building on this;
- finding exceptions to the problem;

- outlining the desired future;
- identifying strengths.

Techniques include:

- scaling questions – to review progress;
- miracle questions – to build a sense of possibility;
- setting small goals – to foster success;
- enlisting the support of others – to clarify boundaries and use resources.

If you are not familiar with this approach for counselling work, you will want to find out more via the suggested reading. However, a short case study follows to illustrate the use of the miracle question and searching for small details to effect change.

Case study 3.2 Nothing I do works with this young person – he is sullen and so de-motivated

The supervisor, Laura: *Suppose for a moment that a miracle had happened since your last meeting with Ben and you meet again and all the problems that you have been telling me about have been resolved. How would you know that had happened – what is the first thing that you'd notice?*

The supervisee, Jem: *Ben would be smiling! No seriously, he would have gone to college, enrolled for a course and be excited about starting. Realistically, it would just be great if he was showing an interest in something.*

Laura: *So what would you be doing if he were showing an interest in something?*

Jem: *Well, I'd be asking him to tell me about his interest, what he liked about it.*

Laura: *So what would be the first sign of this happening – this showing an interest?*

Jem: *Well, the smiling, yes, and actually engaging with me in the session.*

Laura: *Is there something that is already happening that suggests this might be possible?*

Jem: *Hmm, well, he does come for his appointments – never really thought about that in a positive way (pause) – and he does talk sometimes about playing in a band.*

Laura: *What does he play and how does he manage to organise playing with others in a band?*

Jem: *I don't know – we haven't really talked about that. (pause) Yes, I see where you are going with this; he is motivated to play in a band.*

Laura: *Is there anything else you would notice?*

Jem: *Well, if I can engage him through his interests more, he would be talking more openly with me about other things.*

Narrative approaches and supervision

All therapeutic approaches pay attention to the client's story, but to varying degrees. Within narrative therapy and counselling there is recognition that 'telling the story' is not a mere reporting on the facts in order to find solutions. In the telling of the story the teller and the listener are constructing a narrative to help them understand something that happened in the past, through the lens of the present conversation. Such stories are influenced by social context, historical circumstances and culture. Talking about the counselling issue in supervision provides an opportunity for slowing the process down – in other words, taking time to listen to a *re-presentation* that can be heard, explored, challenged, deconstructed and reconstructed in order to gain a new perspective on the issue. Part of the deconstruction is searching for the other voices that may be present in the stories told. Creative methods can be used – including poetry, song and drama – in one-to-one supervision or in groups (see Chapter 8). Using narrative methods can access thoughts and feelings that are repressed and preventing the work with the client from moving forward. Such approaches are creative and enhance reflexivity, but like any challenging intervention need to be agreed to and introduced once rapport has been established. Asking someone new to supervision to express their feelings in a poem may have them heading for the hills in a panic of self-consciousness! A brief, illustrative case study follows, drawing on one narrative technique.

Case study 3.3 I can't find the words to describe how I feel about this client

In a group supervision session, Haroon talked about a client with whom he felt very uncomfortable. His need to demonstrate 'unconditional positive regard' was being severely challenged by this client. The group had used creative approaches before, and they were asked to give their responses in drawings, poems or a short story. The other three group members handed him their 'narrative' responses. One participant wrote a haiku – the few words encapsulated what she sensed that Haroon was feeling.

> Sly, hiding
> A cloaked menace
> With me

To Haroon this was a powerful summary of how he felt when with the client, and it enabled him to accept that his feelings were not 'wrong'. He felt it was okay to acknowledge that the client's behaviour – for which he was attending counselling – was repellent. He realised that his professional 'voice' was suppressing the impact that working with this client was having on him. He said he now felt he could move forward and plan with his supervisor how to continue working with his client.

INTEGRATING APPROACHES

The above models can be used to inform an integrative approach to supervision. An integrative approach will be developmental, but will also provide a structure that combines both skills and process, placing the supervisee at the centre of the work. If we allow for flexibility and the recognition that a 'one size fits all' approach may not be helpful, a range of concepts can be selected and integrated into the approach according to their suitability for the work in hand. However, that selection needs to be thoughtful and grounded in an understanding of the underpinning theory and its appropriateness in particular contexts and with specific individuals.

Westergaard (2006) advocates using an integrative approach for supervision that recognises that each theoretical approach will help to address some, but not all of the aspects that a supervisee is likely to present. The approach can provide a framework within which the functions of supervision can be met. She suggests that Egan's (2007) three-stage model is a useful starting point as it corresponds with the approach that many counsellors use. Egan's model mirrors a recognisable process of problem resolution: identifying the issue; considering options; and planning for change. The simplicity is, of course, seductive and can be overstated: effective use of any approach (in counselling or supervision) is dependent on the careful use of relevant skills and the core attitudes of the counsellor or supervisor, all of which are derived from the person-centred approach of Rogers, i.e. empathy, congruence and unconditional positive regard (1951). There is a danger that any proposed integrative model is treated superficially, and readers not familiar with a three-stage model of helping are recommended to research this further (Egan, 2007; Reid and Fielding, 2007), but moving on, the three stages can be summarised as:

- enabling the client/supervisee to tell the story of 'where they are' at the current time with their 'problem' or a particular case;
- enabling the client/supervisee to explore the options available to resolve the problem/move forward with the case;
- enabling the client/supervisee to suggest, evaluate and plan action for the future.

REFLECTION POINT

Carry out this reflection before continuing to read the text.

What are the issues we need to keep in mind when advocating the benefits of an integrated approach? Reflect on the advantages and disadvantages of combining theoretical approaches for the practice of supervision.

The aim of taking an integrative approach is not to replace existing theories and models with a 'new', singular approach – clearly, this would work against the desire for integration that celebrates the benefits derived from combining diverse methodologies. The aim is to construct a style that fits the particular supervisory relationship, context and issue under discussion. But this cannot amount to a 'pick and mix' approach, where the supervisor just keeps trying a variety of techniques, mined from various theories, until something works. Ethical and effective work requires a developed under-standing of a particular theoretical model and the recognition that sometimes we get it wrong. When that occurs, a supervisor should not carry on regardless, but reflect on what is happening and change the approach. Integration, then, is not a blend where the original concepts are no longer recognisable, and it is not a technical method that fails to go beyond a superficial level of understanding of what is involved. Integration recognises that no one theory can fully explain what it is to be human and that each theory may address some or many, but not all of the facets of human experience – in life, in counselling and also in supervision. In other words, following a single approach can close our minds to the need for openness and flexibility.

As indicated earlier, counselling – or, if preferred in the context of super-vision, communication skills – must accompany the use of any model, and active listening is crucial. To be able to express feelings, thoughts and actions in a relationship of trust enables the supervisee to 'hear' the problem and to reflect, to articulate and to hear their advice to self. This is part of the learning process, and the supervisor, through active listening, facilitates that process. In addition to active listening, the supervisor needs to ask appropriately phrased and challenging questions. Bamber (1998, p42) suggests that at the appropriate point in the relationship, supervisors should ask a number of open questions designed to get the supervisee to consider their internal perceptions within the social context of their practice. The following are examples.

- What did you see?
- What did you feel?
- What did you think?
- What did you do?

The replies will encourage an open conversation that can proceed within a framework that enables the counsellor to explore the supervisee's particular 'frame of reference' (FOR) – in other words, the ways in which they view the situation from their own knowledge and experience. This collaborative approach that acknowledges the 'world views' that influence the work can help both parties to develop understanding and in so doing expose what might be hidden or ignored; identify both internal and external influences on the work; focus on areas where new learning is needed to promote professional development; and relate the issues to theoretical and conceptual knowledge as appropriate (Bamber, 1998; Reid, 2007b).

Harris and Brockbank (2011) have also developed an integrative approach to both psychotherapy and supervision that draws on a range of theories and concepts. They name this the FIT model, which, they say, is founded upon three domains of human functioning.

>   ***F****eeling (F)*
>   ***I****nitiating (or acting) (I)*
>   ***T****hinking (T)*
>
>   (2011, p23)

Like Bamber's questions above, these three domains are grounded in a person-centred approach and incorporate ideas from transactional analysis (TA), Gestalt therapy and cognitive behavioural therapy. CBT has been discussed above and TA is explored further in Chapter 7, but a little will be said now about the FIT model and its use of concepts from Gestalt therapy. Harris and Brockbank's model can be used in supervision to help the counsellor to consider the client's and their own feelings, behaviour and beliefs in relation to their work with the client. Of course, the supervisor can focus on these elements, too, in order to explore their own functioning within the supervisory relationship. The aim is to bring issues that may be in the background into the foreground, where they can be worked on as appropriate. Harris and Brockbank explain the model further:

>   *****F***** *denotes emotions, affect and feelings – material expressed in this domain of the model can be accessed using person-centred, Gestalt and TA techniques*
>
>   *****I***** *denotes initiating, that is, behaviours and actions intimated by the individuals – this domain of the model can be accessed through TA or CBT*
>
>   *****T***** *denotes cognition, thoughts beliefs and self-talk – this domain of the model may be accessed through TA, Gestalt and CBT.*
>
>   (2011, p24)

Space limits further discussion of the model here, but more can be said about the use of a Gestalt technique that can facilitate this awareness-raising in supervision. In German the word Gestalt means 'to give shape or form'. Perls (1972) stated that individuals are not always aware of the feelings and beliefs that shape their lives, and that this can lead them to disown their emotions. Emotional needs may be buried and not recognised, and may be projected on to others. To experience wholeness, these inner conflicts and related emotions need to be expressed in the present to facilitate change and work towards resolution. Gestalt therapy attends to the body as well – not just the mind – and pays attention to the blocks and defences that the mind has suppressed. Gestalt concepts help the supervisee to work primarily with their Feelings (F) by expressing them in the present. The counsellor can explore the interactions that they have with their client in the 'here and now', rather than talking about them in 'there and then'. This helps them to develop their Thinking (T).

The well-known technique of 'the empty chair' is a useful example of Gestalt therapy that can be used in supervision. The supervisee can express their feelings about a client through speaking to the empty chair (as if the client were present). The supervisor and supervisee can pay attention to the feelings expressed in a safe place where these can be discussed further. It may be that the supervisee is projecting material from their own life on to the client, and this may also be playing out in the supervision with the supervisor (this is explored further in Chapter 8). As experienced counsellors will recognise, what is being discussed here are concepts that are informed by psychoanalytical ideas, and these will be introduced next.

DRAWING ON PSYCHODYNAMIC IDEAS FOR SUPERVISION

Ideas from psychoanalytic theory and psychodynamic therapy can help us to think about aspects such as anxiety, defensiveness and unconscious communication that may be taking place within supervision. To clarify, these are not 'negative traits' within an individual or a relational process (such as supervision); exploring them can be beneficial in order to gain a richer understanding of the meanings that are present and influential. There is not enough space here to examine the history of psychoanalytical ideas and their continuing evolution, but they are worth introducing to highlight their explanatory power. In the next section the notions of *anxiety* and *defensiveness* are discussed, before saying a little about the *parallel process*, *transference* and *counter-transference* (the concepts are explored further in later chapters in the book).

ACTIVITY 3.1

Do this activity before reading on.

What is your understanding of the terms written in *italics* above? Could you explain how these relate to supervision?

To aid this activity, try jotting down words or phrases that help to articulate your thoughts.

Anxiety and our defensive strategies

We are all defended subjects as anxiety is part of the human condition. Our defences are there to protect us when we are uncertain or feel threatened, and often these are unconscious responses that affect the way we behave and react to others. Our defensive responses help us to minimise the threat and gain a sense of control over the situation. Reynolds describes these defences:

> *These can include denial, (refusing to accept that something bothers us), projection (attributing feelings or attributes to someone else) and repression (seeking to bury the anxiety as deeply as possible). We have to move beyond the commonplace notion that someone is 'defensive' to understand, initially in ourselves, what this might mean.*
>
> (Reynolds, 2006, pp30–31)

Within supervision we can be challenged by a number of relatively unthreatening issues such as the location, the seniority of the supervisor or the discussion that we are being asked to undertake. But in particular we will be challenged by the difficulty of expressing our feelings of 'stuckness', or incompetence even, when it comes to work with clients. We may hide behind our defences if the supervisory relationship does not provide a safe space to contain and explore these feelings in order to move forward. Such feelings can *evoke 'adolescent' feelings, including a desire to hold on to what may be under threat, and a resistance to change, for fear of the alternative* (Reynolds, 2006, p31).

The parallel process

Westergaard, among others, draws our attention to the 'parallel process' in supervision where *the themes and issues raised in supervision (consciously or subconsciously) often correspond to, reflect or 'parallel' those which are apparent in client case work* (2006, p59). The parallel process is evident when what is occurring in the supervisory relationship parallels or reflects what is taking place in the work between the supervisee and their client. In exploring this, the purpose is to deepen the perception of the supervisee's understanding of the client's needs. The exploration may examine the counsellor's thoughts, feelings and actions towards the client and the counselling relationship, and how these are affecting the relationship within the supervision session. Engaging in this process provides a useful learning opportunity and increases transparency in counselling and supervisory work.

Transference and counter-transference

Closely linked with the parallel process are the concepts of transference and counter-transference. Understanding these unconscious processes can enrich the understanding of counselling work – and, of course, supervision. Transference can take place when something in an interaction triggers a resonance with a past event or relationship – either for the client or for the supervisee. The person can then react to the present situation in the same way that they responded to the past event. In many cases what is evoked is a relationship to an authority figure, but it might also be transference from someone who was very caring – or over-caring. The feelings that might be expressed include anger, hostility, resentment, warmth, love, helplessness and resentment.

Counter-transference refers to the unconscious feelings experienced by the counsellor towards the client. If the counsellor is behaving differently to a particular client than they do towards other clients, counter-transference may be taking place, and this can be explored within supervision. The counsellor can examine their own feelings in relation to the client: for example, why do they feel irritated, bored, sleepy or overwhelmed by this person? Supervision is a place where the unconscious communication taking place in the counselling relationship can be understood and explored in relation to what the client is bringing to counselling that might be causing this. Conversations can then take place regarding how to proceed. These are complex issues that can emerge in relationships with clients and within the supervisory relationship. Engagement with such processes can be stimulating and revealing, and lead to positive learning. However, they can only be fostered within the development of a 'good enough' supervisory relationship – that development is the subject of Chapters 5 to 9.

SPOTTING THE DRAMA TRIANGLE IN SUPERVISION

Before ending this chapter on how theories and concepts can help us to structure supervision, it is useful to consider the drama triangle and supervision – to think about how some of the ideas introduced above can affect the relationship. Drawing on transactional analysis, Hughes and Pengelly (1997) cite the drama triangle as a way of understanding the psychodynamics in supervision when difficulties occur. The drama triangle will be a familiar concept to those engaged in couple counselling: it comprises the roles of *persecutor, rescuer* and *victim*. The classic tale of the Pied Piper of Hamelin is an example of this persecutor-rescuer-victim triangle and demonstrates how the roles are not fixed but can switch.

How does this relate to supervision? A counsellor may have a challenging case where they may be aware that they are trying to rescue the client, who appears to be a victim persecuted by someone else. If the organisation's safeguarding policy means that the counsellor has to report this, they may begin to feel like the persecutor. The counsellor may then turn to the supervisor to be rescued. If the supervisor moves from an empathic understanding to exploring the action, the counsellor may, in turn, feel persecuted by the supervisor and try to cover up the issue, withdrawing from the discussion. The counsellor can feel both persecuted and a victim, and the supervisor might revert to a rescuing role, moving away from issues that need challenging. There can, of course, be variations on this theme. When such occurrences take place, both parties need to think about what is going on and address the problem; otherwise, issues that need to be worked on – in the supervisory relationship and/or in the work with clients – can become too troubling to discuss and ineffective transactions will take place. Using the skill of immediacy and being congruent can help – for example, *I'm not quite sure what is happening, but it seems like* . . . The transference and counter-transference issues can then be discussed as a fruitful way of resolving the issue.

REFLECTION POINT

In your counselling work or in another interaction have you ever experienced the drama triangle? What happened, what did you do, and how did it feel?

LOCATING YOUR THEORETICAL OR CONCEPTUAL POSITION FOR SUPERVISION

Your level of comfort with the final activity in this chapter will depend on many things – for example, your previous or current experience, in terms of both counselling and supervision; the training you have engaged in for either role; the context of your work and the prevailing ethos and discourses that influence it; your culture, age, gender and life experience; and so on. However, it is an important activity if we accept that reflexivity and an ongoing commitment to learning are essential for supervision to be effective, satisfactory to all concerned and even life enhancing.

ACTIVITY 3.2

Look back over the theories and concepts that have been introduced in this chapter. List them as headings and note those that you were already familiar with and those that you were not. Under each heading, write your analysis and evaluation of the theory or concept (albeit this will be short where the explanation here has been brief). An easy way of thinking about analysis and evaluation for this exercise is to ask *What is it about? What seems useful about this? What are my reservations?*

Finally, write a synthesis or summary that indicates where you think you would locate your position with regard to an approach taken to supervision. More than one approach is likely to emerge, but the exercise should help you to reflect on why you have chosen a certain approach or approaches at this point in your thinking about supervision. Anyone who takes an integrated approach needs to know what they are including, where it derived from and why they wish to use it.

The supervisory space can help the counsellor to evolve new approaches alongside maintaining the boundaries of the work, reflecting on the ethical content and expressing their frustrations and anxieties. These activities can be framed within a number of models – theories that can provide a scaffolding as the work develops. The aim of drawing on theoretical concepts is for the supervisee to see the issue with greater clarity and work towards their own conclusions about what might be the 'best' solution. The use of theory gives us tools to think with, helping supervisors to achieve the purpose and functions of supervision in a collaborative manner, thus enabling the supervisee to engage in professional development that becomes genuinely self-motivated. The dialogue that underpins this is more than a cosy chat; it does need a structure, but the structure needs to be both informed and flexible.

Now that we have looked at models, the next chapter will consider methods for implementing supervision.

CHAPTER SUMMARY

This chapter outlined a number of theoretical and conceptual 'maps and models' to frame supervisory practice. It considered:

- developmental and process models;
- aspects of CBT, solution-focused and narrative approaches to supervision;
- integrated approaches;
- ideas from Gestalt and psychodynamic therapy;
- the enactment of the drama triangle in supervision;
- what 'positions' individual perspectives.

SUGGESTED FURTHER READING

Dryden, W (ed.) Counselling in Action series. London: Sage.

The aim of each compact book in this excellent series is to write clear and concise explanations on the range of theoretical and/or conceptual frameworks for counselling. The series also includes texts on other issues and practices relevant to counselling work (e.g. ethics and supervision).

Harris, M and Brockbank, A (2011) *An integrative approach to therapy and supervision: a practical guide for counsellors and psychotherapists.* London: Jessica Kingsley Publishers.

In explaining their integrative model, the authors provide a useful introduction to concepts from person-centred therapy, CBT, Gestalt and transactional analysis, and apply these to supervision. Case studies are included.

Payne, M (2006) *Narrative therapy,* 2nd edition. London: Sage.

A very readable book and illustrated with case studies – a useful introduction to narrative therapy.

Reid, H L and Westergaard, J (2006) (eds) *Providing support and supervision: an introduction for professionals working with young people.* Abingdon: Routledge.

Within this edited text, ideas from psychoanalytical work and solution-focused counselling (among others) and their application to supervision can be explored. Examples for practice are given.

Schuck, C and Wood, J (2011) *Inspiring creative supervision.* London: Jessica Kingsley.

A wonderful book for exploring alternative ways of practising supervision; it also includes explanations of core concepts. In relation to the current chapter, the section on narrative is particularly useful.

CHAPTER 4

Methods for giving and receiving supervision

Hazel Reid

CORE KNOWLEDGE

This chapter will provide the opportunity to:

- evaluate individual supervision;
- consider the advantages and disadvantages of group supervision;
- reflect on alternatives to the 'main' methods of giving and receiving supervision;
- review the need for creativity, alongside considering a cautionary note on the practice of supervision.

INTRODUCTION

As the opening chapters of the book have made clear, supervision is a complex practice, and views about the 'best' method of implementing it are not clear-cut. Much will depend on the nature of the counselling organisation, its purpose and level of funding and the context within which it operates. Personal preferences will also play their part, although these are usually constrained by what is available – albeit that the ideal will always be that methods are negotiated between supervisor and supervisee(s). What follows is an overview of a range of methods – from those that are well established to those that can be viewed as alternative. On the latter, more is said about creative methods in Chapter 8, but an introduction is given here. Finally, the chapter presents a cautionary note on the practice of supervision and asks you to assess its relevance alongside the call for flexibility and creativity.

As part of the supervisory contract, time, frequency, venue, privacy and confidentiality (and its limits) are discussed, alongside the methods to be used. These practical aspects of building a supervisory relationship are so important that they could be discussed next, before proceeding with an exploration of methods for giving and receiving supervision. The details regarding practical arrangements before beginning supervision are discussed in the next chapter. The task in this chapter is to give an outline of methods, with the caveat that more needs to be understood before launching into supervision for the first time. Following on from the chapter on theoretical frameworks, this chapter on methods is perhaps less demanding, and provides a bridge to the focus of the rest of the book.

INDIVIDUAL SUPERVISION

Individual supervision is common in counselling services. It may be referred to as one-to-one or face-to-face supervision, but perhaps the term 'individual supervision' is both more precise and more flexible. Individual supervision may not always be carried out in a room where two people meet face to face, as will be discussed later. It appears obvious that individual supervision is a space for the counsellor/supervisee to focus on their practice: it is, in effect, their time.

REFLECTION POINT

What might interfere with this focus in individual supervision? Imagine this from both sides of the relationship – i.e. as the supervisor and as the supervisee. What can detract from the work, the purpose and functions of supervision as discussed in an earlier chapter? (Perhaps before thinking about this, you might want to review what these are.)

I expect that your thoughts covered both practical issues and relational problems. For example, they may have included relatively minor difficulties related to time and place or significant issues such as a lack of trust or rapport. In turn, these may be linked to your experience and your perceived level of need for supervision. Provided that the working relationship is 'good', then individual supervision does have the potential to ensure that the supervisee's agenda is addressed. But if it is not satisfactory, then the lone supervisee may be reluctant to discuss their practice with the openness that is required, in order to meet the *normative, formative* and *restorative* functions discussed in Chapter 1. If there are problems in the relationship, the supervisee is unlikely to want to discuss areas of difficulty because such exposure may result in viewing these as personal weaknesses or failures. Experiencing a difficulty when working in complex situations with a client is normal practice, not exceptional practice, but this will be hidden rather than revealed if a lack of trust or a power imbalance – or simply a view that they will not be heard by a 'busy' supervisor – is evident. This becomes more serious if there are issues concealed in supervision that are related to the individual's competence to practise.

Case study 4.1 Did I do the right thing?

Sonia is a trainee counsellor who has met with her supervisor, Prem, on several occasions. Although the feedback she gets on her work is good and she is enjoying the counselling work with young people, an experience on the previous day shook her confidence and she is not feeling very secure today about the action she took. She has convinced herself that this is not a child protection or safeguarding issue, but wants to check this with her supervisor. (She has looked at the policy and code of practice, but the situation was not straightforward.) However, she is concerned that bringing it to a supervision session might have a negative effect on Prem's view of her competence. Her supervisory relationship with Prem is okay, but she knows how busy he is and sometimes it is difficult for them both to arrange mutually convenient times to meet.

The supervision session is later today, and Sonia is determined that she will discuss the issue. She then gets a text message from Prem saying that they can still meet but he has to attend an important meeting and he will be delayed by 30 minutes. Prem is delayed for 45 minutes. He apologises to Sonia and says: *What did we say we would focus on in this meeting?* Sonia recognises that Prem is feeling rather stressed and needs to 'get on', so she decides that she'll leave her issue for now and see if there is time before the end of the meeting. She responds to his question with: *Umm, we said we would look at how I am managing my increasing caseload.* They have a useful meeting discussing this, but when Sonia notices Prem looking at his watch, she decides not to open up the subject that is really concerning her. *Maybe next time*, she thinks.

REFLECTION POINT

What are your thoughts on the above? What happened? Why does Sonia decide not to raise the issue?

Sonia has checked out her action against the relevant policy and code of practice, but it looks like she is trying to solve an ethical dilemma, and dilemmas are, inherently, difficult to solve. Her determination to 'reveal' her actions in supervision is thwarted by the delay caused by Prem's 'important meeting'. Will she be thinking, *Isn't our meeting important then?* Or does she just accept that she is less important than this other call on Prem's time? Her supervisor is later than anticipated, and Sonia will have been waiting, perhaps getting more anxious about her action on the previous day. When Prem arrives, he does apologise, but he looks stressed and starts by asking what they agreed last time. *Why doesn't he know what we agreed last time?* she might think. Had she been invited to set the agenda for this meeting, her determination to discuss her concern might have been revived. As it is far easier to hide it for now, it seems better to 'get down to business' and think about it later, maybe. The following chapters discuss how to avoid this unsatisfactory situation, which could potentially be harmful, as the action with the client has not been considered.

There is another point to consider in relation to the barriers for one-to-one supervision being focused solely on the needs of the individual counsellor. Unless a supervisor is external to the organisation, the supervisor cannot remain 'outside' the needs of the organisation, the internal policy demands or the service targets that constrain the work of both supervisor and practitioner. This feature is not limited to line managers who are also supervisors and offering individual supervision to their colleagues. Intrinsically, individual supervision gives a greater degree of confidentiality than group supervision, but where counsellors work in public services, absolute confidentiality cannot be guaranteed. A case study will help to illuminate the complexities around these points.

Case study 4.2 Whose needs are served in supervision?

Jacob is both line manager and supervisor to four members of staff. He talks about his previous experience and his current practice.

Whose needs are served in supervision? That's an interesting question. Before becoming a qualified counsellor, I worked in a guidance organisation helping vulnerable young people. We did not have a system of supervision. It was all very informal – you know, a general conversation with tea and cakes on a Friday afternoon. But sometimes not even that happened because of the demands of the work. There was always someone to see urgently. I was a team leader there, so I always tried to be available to help colleagues – but it wasn't supervision as I now understand it. Anyway, no one was supporting me and it felt like – well, how can I describe it? It felt like I had this backpack that was full of the weight of my own clients' problems, and every time I put it on the floor, someone else would come – another adviser or the centre manager – and put something inside and add to the weight. But I kept picking that backpack up and kept shouldering it! I asked about supervision and they offered me online counselling – I ask you! I said, No thanks – not appropriate!

I then started training part time to be a counsellor, and when I qualified I started working here. I was getting supervision then, and I still do. I really appreciate the support, but also the development and the opportunity to discuss my practice – so beneficial for me and my clients, of course. Once I became a line manager I also started my work as a supervisor. We are a very small organisation and cannot afford external supervision. From my previous experience, I'll always remember what it feels like not to have proper supervision. So, anyway, I would not pretend that it is easy, separating the roles, but I spend a lot of time preparing for supervision and we work together to agree our contract and clarify the boundaries – they have to be clear before you start supervision. We all have many calls on our time – do you know anyone in this type of work who is not busy? No, I thought not! But I take care to give the space and time for supervision meetings, in order to demonstrate the respect to colleagues that I expect them to show to their clients. Yes, I get asked to do other things, but you have to be assertive and protect the time booked and then use it effectively. No one is perfect, and we all have days when we are stressed, but my role as a supervisor is to set other issues aside and listen and work with my supervisee. We cannot ignore organisational imperatives – and paying attention to these is part of my job – but we decide when to discuss this and how. I see all that as part of the collaborative process. Mind you, I would always act if I thought there was a situation that was breaching their professionalism in some unacceptable way – but you can do that in a constructive way.

Me? The centre manager is my supervisor. She has a very small caseload, but it works well. I guess we are both very experienced – mature in that sense. But part of our contract is that we can also discuss my supervision practice when the need arises. I remember once feeling awkward about a counsellor who worked here – nothing concrete but I had misgivings about what they were **not** telling me in supervision – something I knew about from my line manager role. Anyway, with my supervisor we talked this through – the situation, not the person – and agreed the best way forward. I'll not say more, but it worked out well for all concerned. I think I would have probably taken the same action without my own supervision, but it's good to talk! There was trust in me that I would do the right thing, and it helped me to reflect on what that action should be.

I was talking about some of the tensions the other day with one of my supervisees – you know, asking her what she thought about the potential problems of being supervised by her line manager. It was interesting she said that for her it was not a real issue – the trust was there too, I guess. Actually, she said it meant that if she wanted something to change, there was a greater chance it might happen because I **was** a line manager. When I asked her to clarify that, she said that she thought I have the power – ha ha – well, at least access to the resources – to support both her and her clients – within reason, of course! In any event, whoever 'gives' supervision, it will only work if the relationship is good and remains good – you have to work at that in order to meet the needs of **all** concerned.

GROUP SUPERVISION

The other well-known method is group supervision. This can be facilitated by a supervisor – who may be a peer counsellor, someone with particular expertise relating to counselling issues or a counsellor who has completed training as a supervisor – or by the supervision group sharing the task of co-ordinator. At face value, group supervision that is led by a specialist has the advantage of economies of scale, in that a group of practitioners can be supervised together. However, this may result in fewer opportunities to discuss issues or client cases of immediate or particular importance to individual counsellors, which can reduce the perceived value of the method. Setting these reservations to one side, group supervision offers a valuable opportunity to learn from the experience of a number of practitioners, although there is a risk that the more talkative or extrovert counsellor may dominate the space. If the sessions are facilitated by an experienced supervisor, this can be managed effectively to ensure that an equal focus is agreed and maintained. On the other hand, peer group supervision without a specialist supervisor or 'manager' might be viewed as less challenging, enhancing possibilities for the individual to engage more comfortably in *restorative* supervision. The time invested in supervision is a resource that is often in short supply, so both the organisation and the counsellors working in the organisation may be of the view that there are other informal ways that individuals can access additional support. In discussing organised methods, it is important to remember that counsellors will have informal networks that can be used to supplement, but not replace, formal supervision.

ACTIVITY 4.1

Before continuing, spend some time thinking about the advantages and disadvantages of these two established approaches to giving and receiving supervision, using the headings below. Concentrate on your subjective feelings about the two approaches. Be honest rather than striving for the 'correct' answers.

Individual supervision		Group supervision	
Advantages	**Disadvantages**	**Advantages**	**Disadvantages**

My thoughts on this are included at the end of the chapter. (Resist the temptation to look before completing the exercise.) What have you included that did not occur to me?

ALTERNATIVE METHODS FOR GIVING AND RECEIVING SUPERVISION

Within individual and group supervision it is possible to vary the approach by including creative methods for investigating issues brought to the process, and these will be discussed in a moment. First, it is important to acknowledge that there are alternative methods for receiving supervision and that these might be accessed over time as the supervisee develops in experience, knowledge and professional status. For example, methods such as co-supervision with two experienced counsellors engaging in supervision together, case conferences with the involvement of other professionals and peer or collegiate supervision with a group of experienced counsellors all offer alternative forms of supervision to experienced counsellors. However, to return to the subject of creativity in individual and group supervision, the previous chapter referred to the use of the 'empty chair' from Gestalt therapy. It gave an example of using a narrative technique, and Chapter 8 provides further examples. Creative approaches require an element of risk-taking and are dependent on trust within the relationship. Examples can include role play and the use of a dramatic space (i.e. not being fixed to a 'seated' discussion); using diagrams, drawings or graffiti; incorporating the use of colour for expressing aspects of the problem; and using artefacts to represent the 'players' in a situation – for example, through differently shaped pebbles or plastic building blocks.

REFLECTION POINT

What are your initial thoughts on these suggestions? Are there any in particular that you would find interesting or you would find challenging? Why?

Often, in replying to questions about using creative approaches, people will say something like: *I'm not really very creative, so I would find it difficult.* This can be linked to our perception that 'creativity' is about fine art and the ability to draw, the theatre and acting a dramatic part on stage, or crafted materials created through original designs. While these are, clearly, part of an artistic culture, creativity is in all of us, and supervision can be a safe space to play with approaches that engage the imagination and enliven and deepen our understanding of a phenomenon. One way of approaching this in supervision is to be congruent, acknowledge the possibility of embarrassment and say out loud: *I feel a bit uncomfortable with this, but I know this is a safe space to try out new approaches and that I will not be criticised – so I'm prepared to give it a go.* This, or a similar statement, resonates with the discussion in the previous chapter that referred to the concepts of anxiety and defensiveness. Having tried it once, experience and reflection should help to build confidence to develop the approach and experiment with other creative methods. If it does not work, the reasons why it is not effective should be explored.

Where access to supervision is difficult, developing a system 'at a distance' can be a viable option, through using the telephone or other digital technologies. Many counsellors find a reflective journal is helpful for focusing on aspects of their practice in supervision, and this method can be applied 'at a distance'. Similarly, secure discussion groups can be used online. These alternative solutions should not, of course, be viewed as 'quick fix' and 'cheap' solutions when time and other resources are an issue. Whatever the method used, the same careful planning and consultation is required that any process should involve. There are times when supervision is required quickly, but in most cases there is little likelihood of being able to consult a supervisor 'there and then'. In this situation a phone call or email may solve the immediate issue, but for formal supervision to be effective 'at a distance', a range of methods should be contemplated.

Another suggestion is to explore a meaningful process of self-supervision (Morrissette, 2002). Self-supervision recognises that the experienced counsellor can engage in creative reflection on their work, as above, through the use of reflective diaries. Then again, those who already work on their own or in outreach and 'isolated' circumstances may find this simply serves to accentuate their isolation. Nevertheless, where the prospects for engaging in supervision are infrequent, for whatever reason, it is useful to review a combination of methods and to discuss what will match the needs of the supervisee within the available resources. Of course, as suggested in Chapter 1, supervision may not be the only or best way of supporting a practitioner – a short course or consultation with another counsellor who has a particular area of knowledge may be more effective.

ACTIVITY 4.2

Imagine that you are a counsellor who has just started to work in a remote location. Make it very remote – possibly you 'serve' a number of communities on a group of islands that can only be reached by boat. You can decide whether this is the northern hemisphere or a warmer clime. Your employing agency is based on the mainland, which you will visit three times a year. There is no one locally who can offer you supervision. You love your job so far, but you value the supervision that you have always received and your registration states that you must have. How is this going to be organised? Your line manager, on the mainland, has asked you to make suggestions, taking into account the likely costs of the resources involved, the need to be creative and flexible and the availability of technology. You do have electricity, a new laptop computer and broadband connection – although due to the location the electricity supply can be rather vulnerable. (Don't worry if you have based yourself on the Maldives – it happens there as well as on the outer islands in northern parts!)

So while the power's on, write an email to your line manager, outlining a package of what you would like to be implemented and explaining how this will meet your needs, your clients' needs and the needs of the organisation.

Hopefully, you played with the above activity and suggested a mix of methods, drawing on the traditional, alternative and creative suggestions discussed within this chapter.

A CAUTIONARY NOTE ON THE PRACTICE OF SUPERVISION

We would not be writing a book about counselling supervision unless we believed in its value. That said – and as noted previously – it is important to question a taken-for-granted view that supervision is always and forever desired and seen as beneficial by all practitioners. The evidence that supervision improves practice is not easy to find, and Feltham (2002a) suggests that supervision is not accepted as unquestionably necessary or viewed as a 'good thing' by all counsellors. It is generally agreed that it is essential for trainees, but we have to be mindful that experienced counsellors may not always share that view about compulsory supervision. Feltham makes reference to anecdotal evidence of supervisees *feeling cowed, deskilled and wary in relation to supervision, however skilled and ethically competent the supervisor* (2002a, p27).

It is possible that if counsellors take this perspective, they may simply 'play the game' of supervision – 'show up' for the sessions but not engage fully. It is likely that a skilled supervisor would recognise this withdrawal behaviour through attending to the communication that is taking place (see the discussion in Chapter 7 on transactional analysis). However, it would be better to avoid the situation in the first place and ensure that supervision is a collaborative process where models, methods and frequency of meetings are discussed and agreed by all parties involved. If frequency is imposed without a recognition that this can lead to the 'infantalisation' of the counsellor (Feltham, 2002a), then the resulting practice will be perceived as surveillance rather than support. In this regard, there are tensions here between accountability on the one hand and the development of a low-trust, disciplinary surveillance culture on the other (Reid, 2007a). Such ideas draw on the work of Foucault (1979) and how social institutions (and we can include counselling here) *discipline* the behaviour of those who work within them. Supervision, on those terms, is a practice that *governs* counsellors through processes of self-regulation, self-improvement and self-development, which can lead to confessional practices that expose individuals and make them vulnerable. The imperative to engage in supervision takes place within an unequal power relationship: supervision is not a neutral activity. And, where power is present and resented, resistance can be produced: a case study will illustrate this point.

Case study 4.3 Working with resistance in supervision

Pri has been a qualified counsellor for six years and has been supervising for 18 months. She works in a counselling service in a large city alongside eleven other colleagues – all working with clients referred by the regional health authority. Sheila is a counsellor who has recently joined the service on a part-time contract from another area. She is very experienced, well liked and admired for both her practice and her work with students in a nearby university where she lectures two days per week. They meet at a team meeting for the first time, and it is suggested by the service manager that Pri could be Sheila's supervisor. Pri is excited at the idea of being Sheila's supervisor as she read some of her work on psychodynamic counselling when she was training, but she is also a little in awe of her reputation.

They agree a date for a first meeting. Sheila arrives on time and is friendly and courteous to Pri, but the meeting feels rather awkward. Afterwards Pri reflects on the meeting, but cannot work out what was wrong. At the second meeting, arranged within the normal monthly period, Sheila is a little late, apologises, and again, although friendly, Pri gets the sense that she is not engaging with the process. She knows she should challenge this but feels it may be too early to do this. The third meeting is where they should really be developing the supervision of Sheila's counselling, and Pri decides that she must address the relationship issues.

The day of the third meeting arrives, and Sheila is on time but looking a little distracted. Although they had agreed the work they would focus on in this meeting, Pri uses Sheila's apparent distraction as her starting point to address the relationship.

Pri: *I'm wondering if you are OK, Sheila, as you are looking rather distracted.*
Sheila: *Really? No I'm fine, thanks.*
Pri: *Hmm, when I think about our meetings so far, I wonder about our relationship in these sessions – you know, are we building a relationship that will help us in our supervisory work?*

Sheila: *Well now, Pri, what do you mean by that question?*

Pri (smiling): *Well, we both know that for the work to be effective we need to have a good enough relationship, built on trust and confidence in each other's commitment to the work, and at the moment I don't think we have arrived at that point and I'm not sure I understand why. What's your view?*

Sheila: *Yes, I can see why you would be asking yourself that. (pause) I guess I have been going through the motions a bit – please do not see this as a reflection on your work – it's just, well, I'm so busy doing two jobs really, and having to fit these sessions in so regularly alongside everything else is yet another demand on my time.*

Pri: *I understand. So it's the number and regularity of the sessions that is a problem – have I got that right?*

Sheila (pause): *Yes and, well, I suppose a part of me thinks 'For goodness sake! How many times have I been to supervision over the last twenty years – surely I can be trusted to work well!' And I know that is not all that supervision is about, but I'm being honest with you now. It's not that I think my work should not be supervised – heavens above, I talk to students about its importance. But, I don't know, I guess your challenge has made me realise I need to think about this more (laughs) – and I'm supposed to be a reflector!*

Pri: *Yes, but we know it's always difficult to see ourselves; and twenty years is a lot of supervision sessions! Always individual – or group supervision as well?*

Sheila: *Normally individual, although I have had group supervision from time to time, and I liked the mix of the two in one place where I worked.*

Pri: *That's got me thinking, Sheila. We have to meet the requirements of our organisation, but I wonder if we could think about using different methods in our supervision sessions. The other day I was reading a book about creative approaches. Perhaps we could think about designing our sessions to incorporate various methods and approaches – structuring our time in different ways.*

Sheila: *It's a possibility, provided we both agree on what the approaches are.*

Pri: *Of course, we must both feel comfortable in what we do and accept that we might not get it right on the first attempt – we'd be experimenting together.*

Sheila: *Yes. Like the sound of that – when I think about it more now, I have become bored with the same old ways of doing supervision. What shall we try first?*

Pri (laughing): *Now you've put me on the spot! I've no doubt with your expertise you have used Gestalt and role play before. For the next session, how about we try using artefacts to represent the counselling and the players within the relationships. We could use toy animals and bricks – I'll raid my children's toy box! The bricks can help us to place the characters at different levels. The animals can help us to consider characteristics that we ascribe to individuals, that we may not have thought about before. My reading suggests this can help us to explore our thoughts from another perspective, rather than 'just' talking about the counselling. It can add variety and depth to the process.*

Sheila: *Sounds interesting – we'll give it a go. When shall we meet again to do this?*

Pri: *Well, let's find a date in a minute. The other thing we could also consider is whether we always have these meetings here, or if there are alternative ways of engaging in supervision . . .*

Sheila: *I would like to try writing a reflective journal and sharing that with you.*

Pri: *Great! Well, let's think about how we could work with that idea too.*

Alongside recognising and respecting Sheila's experience and autonomy, Pri is demonstrating the skill of immediacy in the above, in order to challenge what she perceives as a barrier to establishing a working relationship with Sheila. Using these skills in supervision is discussed further in Chapter 8.

A balance needs to be found between respecting counsellors' professionalism and autonomy, and avoiding complacency, arrogance and the potential of inappropriate or even dangerous behaviour in counselling. It has already been stated that the relationship in supervision (as in counselling) is fundamental in terms of its effectiveness. However, that focus can lead to 'collegial cosiness' (Feltham, 2002b: 333). To avoid this, finding a mix of methods and creative ways of engaging in supervision can be the answer – as advocated in this chapter. Feltham (2002a) goes further and suggests that we should recognise that some practitioners may practise best without supervision and could be allowed to take a break from supervision, or, more radically, stop altogether after a period of five or ten years.

Stopping supervision altogether would not be permitted within registered counselling practice in the UK (BACP, 2010) and would not be a course of action that the authors of this book would advocate. In our research, mentioned in the introductory chapter and the focus of the final chapter, none of our participants spoke against the practice: all viewed it as a necessary part of their professional lives. But the costs of providing and receiving supervision for an organisation, or an individual, cannot be ignored, and the process for implementing this effectively needs to be evaluated and reviewed. Thus cautionary tales alert us to the possibility that some counsellors may be resistant to continuous supervision, particularly where they feel the style and/or quality of the practice is imposed, not helpful or not relevant for them. Flexibility, alongside a collaborative approach that is sensitive to the issues discussed in this section, appears to be essential for effective supervision to be achieved by all its intended beneficiaries.

ACTIVITY 4.3

But what do you think? What might be the circumstances that would lead you to consider that supervision was no longer useful? Summarise your views about:
a) the compulsory requirement for supervision and its disciplinary nature; and
b) the call that this chapter has made for creativity in terms of methods and flexibility. One or two sides of A4 paper will be enough to help you process the ideas that have been outlined in this chapter.

CHAPTER SUMMARY

This chapter has focused on methods for giving and receiving supervision. It has examined:

- aspects of individual supervision;
- the advantages and disadvantages of group supervision;
- alternatives to the 'main' methods of giving and receiving supervision;
- the need for creativity and flexibility in our approaches to the practice;
- the need to question our assumptions that supervision is always valued.

You will be ready now to explore the process for supervision, starting with Chapter 5, which discusses the importance of preparation in order for the relationship to be developed and for the work to be effective.

My attempt at Activity 4.1

Individual supervision		Group supervision	
Advantages	**Disadvantages**	**Advantages**	**Disadvantages**
Time to focus on my needs/cases	Always 'under the spotlight'	More sharing – can feel more comfortable and less challenging	Can be dominated by those with more to say
Time to look in depth at any issue	Must always be fully prepared	Can learn from others' experience and difficulties	Limited time to focus on my needs/cases
Feels more confidential	Might say more than I mean to – can feel a bit like a need to 'confess'	Feels collegiate	Difficult to arrange mutually convenient times
Can be continual – not starting from scratch each time	Might get stuck in the same way of doing things	Counters a feeling of being isolated at times – can hear about issues experienced by others	Will have to explain my work more frequently – no one-to-one relationship with my supervisor
Feedback can be shared in each session	Not getting a range of views, as just two people in the relationship	Opportunity to try a different method and practise group skills	Might be asked to engage in activities that I am not comfortable with
Can be arranged within my work schedule	We have to work hard at the relationship	Where funding is limited, can ensure we get supervision	Danger that it is seen as a replacement for more in-depth supervision
It's a relationship that can develop really well between two people	Not getting an opportunity to learn from others	I can listen more – the spotlight is not always on me	Less confidential

SUGGESTED FURTHER READING

Feltham, C (2010) *Critical thinking on counselling and psychotherapy.* London: Sage.

Feltham's writing is always thought provoking – challenging counsellors to question their practice and its place within social structures. The references in the chapter relate to his work on supervision, and Feltham has written other text books on supervision – but this book is an essential read for the promotion of critical thinking.

Hawkins, P and Shohet, R (2012) *Supervision in the helping professions,* 4th edition. Maidenhead: Open University Press/McGraw Hill.

As noted previously, an excellent handbook. We have used the third edition in our work, but the latest, fourth edition has additional contributions and would be the edition to access for the authors' latest revisions and updates on theories, models and methods.

Schuck, C and Wood, J (2011) *Inspiring creative supervision.* London: Jessica Kingsley Publishers.

Although recommended previously, this book appears again in this list as it provides inspiration for finding alternative methods that help to refresh supervision. It offers clear explanations for using a wide range of interesting techniques.

PART TWO

CHARTING THE DEVELOPMENT OF THE SUPERVISORY RELATIONSHIP

CHAPTER 5

Preparing for supervision

Jane Westergaard

CORE KNOWLEDGE

This chapter will provide the opportunity to:

- identify what needs to happen *before* the supervisory relationship is established;
- clarify the responsibilities of supervisor and supervisee *prior* to commencing a supervisory relationship;
- establish key planning issues and practicalities, including organisational issues, policy context, time/frequency of supervision, venue and record keeping.

INTRODUCTION

> *A strong supervisory relationship based on trust and respect is vital to the supervisee's exploration of personal and professional issues that affect supervision and work with clients.*
>
> (Muse-Burke et al., 2001, p32)

As the quote above suggests, it is the development and maintenance of the *relationship* between supervisor and supervisee that is paramount to the effectiveness of the supervision process (Green, 2010). So far in this book, key concepts, theories and ideas concerning what makes effective supervision for counsellors have been examined. But throughout, emphasis has been placed on the part that the supervisory relationship plays in determining the effectiveness of supervision. And as authors of a book entitled *Effective Supervision for Counsellors*, we have a responsibility to explore this relationship further. So it is the development of the relationship between supervisor and supervisee and the *application* of the theories and concepts discussed earlier in the book that will be examined in depth in this chapter, and the four chapters that follow.

Unsurprisingly, the supervisory relationship has been scrutinised in the literature (Stoltenberg and Delworth, 1987; Feltham and Dryden, 1994; Holloway, 1995; Hawkins and Shohet, 2006; Inskipp and Proctor, 2009; Davys and Beddoe, 2010), and a range of models and frameworks have been developed that chart its progress. Holloway (1995) identifies three phases to the supervisory relationship, which are:

- the beginning phase;
- the mature phase;
- the terminating phase.

This is a helpful starting point and provides a simple but clear model that maps the stages through which the relationship progresses. But if the relationship is to be examined in depth, this developmental process needs to be broken down further to include a point *before* the relationship has formed and to chart the characteristics of what Holloway names the 'mature phase' in more detail. The model described here comprises five stages, which are:

- preparing for supervision;
- establishing an effective supervisory relationship;
- progressing the supervisory relationship;
- working at depth, maintaining a working alliance in supervision;
- ending the supervisory relationship.

The stages outlined above are not linear but cyclical, as for many counsellors and supervisors the process of supervision will continue even when the relationship with a current supervisor comes to an end. Ending supervision with one supervisor is likely to result in preparing for supervision with another, and thus the process of developing a supervisory relationship begins again.

So from this point onwards in the book there is a shift in emphasis, and the *chronology* of the process of supervision and the development of the supervisory relationship will be 'put under the microscope' from a point before the supervisor and supervisee meet together for the first time to the moment when the supervisory relationship comes to an end. Chapters 5 to 9 set out to explore the stages of development of this relationship from the perspective of both supervisor and supervisee. The ideas and concepts introduced earlier in the book will be applied to the actual practice of supervision as it develops.

This chapter focuses on stage one of the model: preparing for supervision. It sets out key tasks prior to supervision taking place and examines the systems that should be attended to in order to support the process. In addition, the chapter establishes the practical details of supervision: where, when, how often and so on.

Three case studies are introduced that will be continued in the four subsequent chapters in order to examine how effectively the relationship between each supervisor and supervisee develops.

WHY THE NEED TO PREPARE FOR SUPERVISION?

It may seem strange that we begin our focus on the development of the supervisory relationship by examining what happens *before* either party meets together for the first time. But it is important to be aware of the role that good preparation plays in enabling supervision to get off to a positive start.

ACTIVITY 5.1

Think back to your first supervision as a counsellor. Note down all the things that you think had to happen in order that the meeting between you and your supervisor could take place. Remember that as well as the practicalities (a room, for example) there would have been other elements for your supervisor to prepare. And what about you, as a supervisee? How did you prepare for this experience? If you have not yet received supervision, think about what you know about the process so far, and consider the things that you might need to prepare in order to use the session effectively.

Of course, your response to the activity above will depend on a number of factors. First, what was the organisational context for your counselling practice at the time? Or what is it now if you are a new supervisee? For example, it is likely that the first experience of supervision is as a trainee counsellor undertaking a placement in a counselling agency, and if this is the case, the system of supervision offered by that agency will influence your reflections. Second, the *role* of your first supervisor will have an impact on the preparation required. For example, if your first supervisor is part of the organisation or even your line manager, preparation will include elements not required if your supervisor is someone external to the organisation. Third, the method of supervision will influence the preparation. If, for example, your first supervision session is as part of a group, preparation will include tasks not necessary for an individual meeting. Whatever the system of supervision, role of your supervisor and method employed, your list is likely to include some or all of the following.

- Practicalities – preparation of the supervision environment, arrangements for date, time and duration of first session.
- Knowledge – understanding of theories and processes underpinning supervision, clarity about supervision policy (confidentiality, for example) and boundaries, familiarity with record keeping.

- Skills – development of key supervisory skills to ensure the effective establishment of the relationship.

If one or more of these elements is missing, there is likely to be an impact on the establishment of a meaningful supervisory relationship when supervisor and supervisee *do* first meet together. Without adequate preparation a number of elements are at risk. First, if practicalities have not been attended to, both supervisor and supervisee may not be clear about where, when and how supervision is taking place. At a time when both participants are likely to experience levels of anxiety about this new relationship, difficulties and confusion concerning practical aspects do not help. We would not expect clients to be unsure about their first counselling appointment in terms of when it is, where it is and how long it will last, and the same is true for supervision.

Second, without adequate levels of knowledge regarding the purpose, functions, processes, boundaries and tasks of supervision, the supervisor is unlikely to feel confident about their role and their ability to supervise effectively. Not only do supervisors need to develop an understanding about supervision practice and its theoretical underpinning; they are also required to be clear about the organisational, legal and ethical responsibilities of the role. In the same way, counsellors must attend to these issues in their counselling practice with clients.

Third, supervision, like counselling, requires the development of foundation and advanced skills whereby the relationship can be established and maintained effectively, and the restorative, normative and formative functions can be addressed (Inskipp and Proctor, 1993).

In most cases supervisors will have a counselling background and therefore already have grounding in counselling skills and techniques. This is helpful when addressing the restorative function, where the same skills are applied in the supervision context. However, Holloway suggests that supervising trainee counsellors is *a formal relationship in which the supervisor's task includes making judgements of trainees' performance* (normative function) and *imparting expert knowledge* (1997, p251), in order to meet the formative function. 'Making judgements' and 'imparting expert knowledge' are not activities that normally feature in a counselling relationship, and supervisors will therefore need to develop and hone skills in order to do this effectively.

What follows is a brief examination of the key elements that both supervisors and supervisees need to attend to and prepare, prior to supervision taking place.

PREPARING FOR SUPERVISION: THE PRACTICALITIES

Hawkins and Shohet point out that *it is necessary to be clear about the practical arrangements such as the times, frequency, place, what might be allowed to interrupt or postpone the session, and clarification of any payment that is involved* (2006, p64). As suggested above, without appropriate practical arrangements in place, supervision is unlikely to get off to the best start. So what is required in order that both supervisor and supervisee can feel confident that practical issues have been attended to? The list below suggests the key practicalities to consider.

- A comfortable, private and confidential space should be available and set up appropriately.
- A time should be set aside for supervision.
- Both supervisor and supervisee should be notified about attendance prior to the first supervision session.
- Any payment should be clarified prior to the first meeting.

Case study 5.1 demonstrates what can happen when these practical arrangements have not been prepared adequately.

Case study 5.1 Carole: supervisor

I'd been supervising for an organisation for some time and all the practicalities of supervision were 'sorted' for me. I had a private and confidential room booked in advance, no interruptions, and there was no question of dealing with payment. I never had to think about it – because someone else had!

Then I took on a private counselling supervisee, and I realise now that I just didn't attend to the practicalities properly. For a start, I agreed that supervision could take place in my supervisee's home. This was a disaster. I began by arriving late because I couldn't find her house. Once started, we were constantly distracted by her young children running around and playing upstairs. The room was simply not conducive to this kind of interaction. The phone rang more than once during the session, as did the doorbell. Horrendous! Added to which, I found it really difficult when the time came to end the session and ask for my fee. On top of that, I really didn't know how to respond when my supervisee took out her diary and asked when I would be coming again! If I'd taken a bit more time to think the practicalities through and prepare properly, things would have been very different.

Carole's experience highlights the importance of ensuring that the practicalities of supervision have been attended to in order that the environment is suitable for establishing a supervisory relationship. It may well be that, as in Carole's case, you begin supervising for an organisation and practical aspects are dealt with for you. This is helpful. But even where this is the case, it is worthwhile familiarising yourself with your surroundings in order to feel confident and comfortable with the environment in which you will be engaging in supervision.

Helpfully, the British Association for Counselling & Psychotherapy issues guidance on supervision, in particular the issue of 'how much' supervision counsellors should have (Mearns, 2008). This guidance recognises the importance of supervision in maintaining quality in counselling practice. It stipulates that in order for counsellors to achieve and maintain accreditation they are required to undertake one and half hours of individual supervision (or equivalent) a month for each month that counselling takes place. Any supervisor or counsellor new to supervision should access this guidance before their first supervision session. Those entering private practice must research and determine their fee level by checking what is generally the 'going rate' demanded by supervisors.

PREPARING FOR SUPERVISION: THE KNOWLEDGE

While preparing the practicalities is relatively straightforward and the list of 'things to do' is not too onerous, the knowledge needed to undertake supervision is more complex to develop. On a positive note, new supervisors will have received supervision themselves as counsellors, so they will be aware of what the process involves and the wealth of expertise that the supervisor brings. A new or trainee counsellor experiencing supervision for the first time would also benefit from knowing what is involved and what supervision sets out to achieve. It is easy to forget, once familiar with supervision, how daunting that first-ever session can be.

It may help to reduce anxiety for new counsellors if – *prior* to supervision taking place – they have some knowledge of what supervision is all about and what is likely to happen in sessions. To think about this further it is helpful to divide knowledge into more specific categories.

- Supervision – purpose, function and tasks.
- Theoretical orientation – supervisor's and supervisee's.
- Principles of reflective, reflexive and anti-oppressive practice.
- Organisational policy and legal aspects – for example, attendance, record keeping, limits of confidentiality.
- Ethical aspects – for example, boundary setting, contact outside supervision session.

The wealth, depth and breadth of knowledge required before supervision can take place might at first sight appear overwhelming. But, as mentioned previously, those who become supervisors are likely to have gained much of this knowledge already, both through their counselling practice and through their own experience of being supervised. They will be aware of the purpose of supervision, and they will have been trained in and applied a particular theoretical orientation in their counselling practice. They will have developed as reflective and reflexive practitioners, and they will have an understanding of policy and requirements for legal, ethical and boundaried working with clients. That said, preparing for supervision is not as simple as saying *I've had it, so now I can do it.* By contrast, counsellors who are about to receive supervision for the first time will not have the benefit of specific experience on which to draw, but they will be familiar with the supportive relationships they have made already with their tutors and fellow students in training, and this should prove useful.

ACTIVITY 5.2

Using the headings in the grid below and reflecting back on your reading in Part One of the book, note down the specific knowledge about supervision that you already have. It might help to begin by identifying knowledge in relation to your counselling practice/training before reflecting on this knowledge with regard to the activity of supervision.

Knowledge	New supervisor	New supervisee
Supervision purpose, function and tasks	What are your own experiences of supervision? What did you get out of the relationship? What *should* supervision set out to achieve?	What do you think supervision is all about? What would you like it to do?
Theoretical orientation	What is your own counselling orientation? (For example, is it person-centred, integrative, psychodynamic?) How might this have an impact on supervision? And what if your supervisee has been trained in a different approach to your own?	What is your counselling orientation? (For example, are you training in person-centred, integrative, psychodynamic or other approaches?) How might supervision help you to develop your knowledge and understanding of these approaches and conceptualise them in your work with clients?

Knowledge	New supervisor	New supervisee
Principles of reflective, reflexive and anti-oppressive practice	How has your own supervision helped you to develop skills of reflection? How reflexive is your practice? What has been your experience of (anti-)oppressive practice in supervision?	How might supervision help you to reflect on your practice? What does being a reflexive practitioner mean? What is your understanding of anti-oppressive practice and how might it be relevant to supervision?
Organisational policy and legal aspects – for example, attendance, record keeping, limits of confidentiality	What is your understanding of the organisation's policy on supervision and the legal aspects of supervision from your own experience? How often did you attend supervision? What records were kept? Who had access to them? What were the limits of confidentiality in your supervision sessions?	First, think about your understanding of the organisation's policy on counselling practice and the legal aspects of counselling work with clients. What are the procedures for record keeping and what are the limits of confidentiality in counselling practice? Now think about how this might parallel what happens in supervision.
Ethical aspects – for example, boundary setting, contact outside supervision session	What contracts have been agreed in supervision? What do they contain? What are the boundaries of your relationship with your supervisor? How effectively has this worked for you?	Again, think first about what you already know about counselling practice with clients. Why do counsellors agree contracts with clients? Why are boundaries important in counselling? How might this apply to supervision too?

This is a challenging activity. However, if completed fully, it demonstrates that there is already much that you know about the process, whether you have received supervision or you are training to be a counsellor but are new to supervision. What follows is a brief overview of each 'category' of knowledge. Much of what is needed here has already been written about in previous chapters in this book, and where this is the case, I will signpost appropriately. The purpose of this and the four subsequent chapters, as explained earlier, is to help you to *apply* the knowledge you already have, as well as integrate new understanding *in practice*.

Supervision – purpose, functions and tasks

McMahon (2002) suggests three conceptualisations underpinning supervision: a relationship; a developmental process; and a learning environment. These resonate with Inskipp and Proctor's functions of supervision mentioned earlier in the chapter: formative; normative; and restorative. Case study 5.2 shows how a lack of understanding about the purpose of supervision can leave a new counsellor with unnecessary anxiety.

Case study 5.2 Lucy: counsellor

It was silly really, looking back, but I remember being almost paralysed by fear when I went to my first supervision session. I was young, had no experience, and I had no idea what to expect. As I sat in the waiting area, it felt to me like sitting outside my head-teacher's office, waiting to be told off. I kept telling myself that supervision wouldn't be like that, but I didn't really know for sure. When I was called in, my palms were sweating and my voice came out as a whisper. I needn't have worried. My supervisor was great! When I think back, it makes me smile to remember how I was then.

Perhaps if Lucy had had a clearer idea about what supervision was all about prior to engaging in the process, her fears would have been less overwhelming. To summarise, the purpose of supervision is to attend to the support, development and practice of the counsellor for the benefit of the client. As Reid (2006) suggests, supervision is all about taking care of self in order to take care of others. By understanding this at the outset, those who are new to supervision, either as a supervisor or as a supervisee, can approach their first session with a new supervisor/supervisee confident that there is a shared and common purpose.

Theoretical orientation

It is important to acknowledge that the theoretical orientation – the approach that counsellors are trained in and use with clients – of both supervisor and supervisee is likely to have an impact on supervision. Case study 5.3 illustrates this clearly.

Case study 5.3 Phil: counsellor

I had a supervisor a few years ago who was a pure person-centred therapist. I have to say that sometimes I found this frustrating when it came to supervision. I'm trained as an integrative counsellor, and although I understand and integrate the core conditions of person-centred work in my approach with clients, I found the focus on the 'here and now' in supervision difficult sometimes. In some ways, there were positives to be gained. I became a more reflective practitioner, I think. But there was little space to discuss other aspects of practice. I remember wanting to talk about using CBT techniques with a particular client, and my supervisor just seemed to raise his eyebrows and look slightly concerned. I didn't find this particularly helpful.

Although Phil's testimony raises some questions about working with different counselling theoretical orientations in supervision, it should not act as a warning against two people working together where their training and practice is based in contrasting therapeutic approaches. In fact, it is possible and even desirable that supervision is enhanced by engaging with and valuing different perspectives. Lizzio and Wilson explain:

> *The challenge for supervisors is to approach the conceptualisation of practice in a way that helps supervisees integrate these aspects of knowing. Clearly, supervision must not only address the task of assimilation (of applying existing theory to practice) but also of accommodation (developing new theory or personal theory from practice).*
>
> (Lizzio and Wilson, 2002, p33)

It is the responsibility of the supervisor to be aware of their own counselling theoretical orientation and to reflect on how this may inform the process of supervision. They should be cognisant of the need to respond to their supervisee in a way that is helpful and enabling. It is, after all, the development of the supervisee as a counsellor, working with clients, that is at stake here.

So, before supervision takes place for the first time, a new supervisor should examine their own philosophy and theoretical underpinning to counselling and, therefore, their supervision practice. They should ask themselves how they would respond to working with a supervisee who does not share their approach. A new supervisee should also reflect on their own training and practice so that if they are in a position to choose their supervisor, they may decide to look for someone with a compatible theoretical orientation to their own. They can then engage in their first supervision session with confidence, ready to begin to articulate and conceptualise, as far as they can, their emerging counselling perspective.

Principles of reflective, reflexive and anti-oppressive practice

Before engaging in supervision, both supervisor and supervisee should be clear about the part that reflection plays in order to develop as reflexive counsellors (Schön, 1983; Boud et al., 1985; Scaife, 2010). In addition, anti-oppressive practice (Thompson, 1993) must be central to the supervisory relationship, and, again, both supervisor and supervisee would do well to give some time to considering issues of possible oppression within the relationship before they meet together. The concepts of reflective, reflexive and anti-oppressive practice are discussed more fully in Chapter 2. Here, the focus is on helping supervisors and supervisees to prepare for supervision by reminding themselves of the significance of each. In Case study 5.4, Carl, a new supervisor, describes his first supervision session, where, on reflection, oppression may have been an issue.

Case study 5.4 Carl: supervisor

I suppose I should have given it more thought. But because I was so anxious, given that it was my first supervision experience as a supervisor, I went into the session wanting to be really helpful. I think two things happened. First, I ended up dominating the session and 'advising' instead of enabling the supervisee to reflect on her work with clients. Second, as my supervisee was so new to counselling, a lot younger than me and our social and cultural backgrounds were so different, I picked up issues there that I don't think I handled well. There was definitely some tension in the room. And I know that I came across more and more as an 'expert' telling my supervisee what she should do. I think, on reflection, it's quite possible that my supervisee felt oppressed. And I was too nervous myself to notice or do anything about it at the time.

Carl reminds us that the purpose of supervision is to encourage reflection on behalf of the supervisee in order to develop good counselling practice. It is not about 'providing answers' even if supervisees new to the process appear to be seeking them. It is important to recognise the power of transference and counter-transference here and to be alert to it at all times in supervision, but particularly early on in the relationship with a new and inexperienced supervisee (there is more on this in later chapters as the developing relationship is examined in more detail). Perhaps Carl was responding to the subconscious need from his supervisee for authority, forgetting momentarily that his role was to encourage her to reflect on practice and find her own answers. It may also be, as Carl suggests, that his supervisee felt oppressed in the relationship. This was not something that Carl set out to do, but was an unconscious process informed by age, gender, and social and cultural factors.

By reminding ourselves of the centrality of reflective and reflexive practice in supervision, and the significance of developing an anti-oppressive relationship with supervisees, we can prepare ourselves to engage in the work. Shohet and Wilmot summarise:

> *Thus race, age, sex, ideology, boundaries, power, control, confidentiality could all be, and often are, issues. However, as long as the two parties see it as their priority to explore the process of their working together, then the issues are in effect vehicles by which they can do this (and are therefore to be welcomed).*

> (Shohet and Wilmot, 1991, p88)

Prior to supervision taking place, both supervisee and supervisor should take some time to reflect on these key concepts. As reflexive practitioners they should be aware of the importance of the reflective process and the role that supervision has in developing their own skills of reflection. They should be cognisant too of the part that social, gender, cultural, ethnic and other factors can play in the development of any relationship. If they are prepared to discuss this openly in supervision, then possible issues of oppression in the relationship can be recognised and dealt with appropriately.

Organisational, policy and legal aspects

Chapters 2 and 4 of this book provide a sound introduction to the organisational, policy and legal aspects of supervision. Furthermore, Jenkins (2001) offers a detailed account of supervisory responsibility and the law, and Mitchels and Bond (2010) provide in-depth guidance on the law for counselling and psychotherapy. Clearly, the context in which supervision takes place is likely to have a significant impact on the amount of preparation required in relation to developing knowledge on policy and legal issues. If supervisors are working for an organisation rather than in private practice, for example, detailed, specific policies should be in place for systems such as record keeping and the boundaries of confidentiality. It is, of course, the responsibility of the organisation to be clear and transparent concerning these aspects of supervisory practice with the new supervisor. Moreover, it is important for supervisors to familiarise themselves with these policies prior to supervision taking place. By so doing, when they are establishing a relationship and agreeing a contract for supervision with their supervisee (see Chapter 6), they can be confident about the legal and policy requirements of the role. In the next case study Balvinder explains how knowledge of her organisation's policies prior to supervision averted a potentially difficult situation in an early session with a new supervisee.

Case study 5.5 Balvinder: supervisor

My supervisee explained that the work she was currently doing with one of her clients was raising some challenging issues for her because of her own past experience of mental health issues. She asked me if it was 'safe' to talk about her own 'stuff' as she didn't want the counselling organisation to know about this aspect of her personal history. I was so pleased that I'd checked out fully the organisation's policy on confidentiality and data protection so that I could be clear with my supervisee about what I could and couldn't divulge in my notes.

It would not be helpful to set out here a full and detailed analysis of the boundaries of confidentiality and data protection or other legal aspects in counselling supervision (Bond and Mitchels, 2008; Mitchels and Bond, 2010). That is partly because these issues are something of a 'movable feast', given that the law can change. But, more importantly, it would be unhelpful to establish a set of rules or even guidelines, as the context within which counselling and supervision take place will determine, to a large extent, the policy concerning confidentiality.

For example, a supervisor supervising counsellors who work with children, young people or vulnerable adults will be governed by legal and policy restrictions not necessarily duplicated in couple counselling. There is a further responsibility here for supervisors who are operating in private practice. These individuals do not have the backing of an organisation to support their practice. It is therefore imperative that they take responsibility for accessing current, relevant literature on the policy and legal requirements of supervision and use their own supervision as well as professional organisations such as the BACP to support and inform their practice.

Jenkins summarises the potential challenge of negotiating the legal responsibilities for supervisors:

> *Supervisors carry a range of legal responsibilities to their supervisee, to the client and to their employing organisation. The exact nature of their responsibilities will vary according to their employment status, the nature of their contract with the supervisee and any contract with their own agency.*
>
> (Jenkins, 2001, p38)

Suffice to say that the organisational, policy and legal requirements of supervision should be embedded before the first supervision session with a new supervisee takes place. Furthermore, supervisors have a responsibility to keep their knowledge current, and their own supervision will provide a forum to examine the application of policy and the law in detail in their practice.

Ethical aspects of supervision practice

All counsellors – in training or in practice – will be aware of the significance of working ethically in their relationships with clients. They will not be surprised, then, to discover that ethical working is as central to supervision as it is to counselling practice. Ethical working is discussed in detail in Chapter 2 of this book and is outlined in depth in the BACP code of practice (2010). The intention in this chapter is not to replicate what has gone before, but to consider why it is necessary for supervisors to remind themselves of the importance of ethical practice in supervision *before* they engage in a supervisory relationship. Case studies 5.6 and 5.7 demonstrate the importance of understanding what ethical practice means in supervision *prior* to supervision taking place.

Case study 5.6 George: supervisor

I wasn't really sure what to do when my supervisee began to call me at home. I'd given her my home number and explained that she could use this in emergencies, but I don't think, reflecting back, that I was clear enough about the boundaries of our relationship at the outset. I'm not sure that I even knew what they were myself! She called me frequently about what seemed to me to be fairly straightforward aspects of her practice. The problem was that I didn't challenge this behaviour early enough and we reached a point where I felt that whatever I said would be misconstrued and could potentially damage our relationship. To crown it all, on one occasion, at the end of a call, my supervisee asked me if I would like to go to a party she was having at her house. This completely floored me!

Case study 5.7 Charlene: supervisor

When I first decided to train as a supervisor in the same organisation that I'd been working in for many years as a counsellor, I was clear that I did not want to supervise colleagues who I'd worked alongside as a counsellor and socialised with. The organisation was fine about that and agreed to support my request. I now only supervise new or trainee counsellors, and I don't supervise any of my old colleagues or friends. For me, it just wouldn't be ethical. I'm sure that it is possible and that it happens and probably some people manage it really well. But it wouldn't have been right for me and it would have had an impact on my practice.

Both case studies highlight the intensely personal nature of ethical practice. Working ethically in counselling and supervision means adhering to a set of principles (BACP, 2010), including fidelity, autonomy, beneficence, non-maleficence, justice and self-respect; every counsellor and supervisor has to make ethical judgements about their practice at times, and these decisions are often subjective. For example, in George's case study, the lack of establishing and adhering to clear boundaries in supervision has put the ethical principles of autonomy, beneficence and justice at risk. If George had spent time with his supervisee setting out clearly both the circumstances where it might be appropriate to contact him between sessions and the boundaries of this professional relationship, then this situation might have been avoided. Charlene, by contrast, is anxious to ensure that she adheres to the principle of non-maleficence in her supervision practice, and she fears that her relationships with supervisees who are already friends and close colleagues would not be tenable.

ACTIVITY 5.3

If you are new to becoming a supervisor, then it might be helpful to reflect back on the ethics of your relationship as a counsellor with your own supervisor/s. Consider situations in the past that may have posed ethical dilemmas for your supervisor. It could also help to ask yourself hypothetical questions that you can take to your organisation or to your own supervisor to discuss further. For example, what might you do if:

- you are attracted to your supervisee?
- your supervisee is a former counselling client who has now trained as a counsellor?
- your supervisee asks to finish supervision early on frequent occasions?
- your supervisee asks to meet with you outside of supervision, 'just for a coffee and a chat'?
- your supervisee asks you to complete a reference for a counselling position in another agency?
- your supervisee asks you to falsify the number of supervision sessions they have attended in the year by one or two in order to keep their BACP accreditation?

This is just a sample of possible ethical issues, and, of course, there are others not detailed here. By reflecting on what *could* present an ethical dilemma in supervision before embarking on a supervisory relationship, the supervisor is best placed to respond appropriately if an ethical challenge should arise. The need for reflection-in-action is clear in these situations. A response that 'buys time' is helpful so that the supervisor can consider the issue and take their concerns to their own supervision.

PREPARING FOR SUPERVISION: THE SKILLS

The good news for new supervisors is that they will, in most cases, transfer the skills they have developed as a counsellor to a different, but related, context. These skills include:

- active listening – using all senses to attend to what is being said, how it is being said and, importantly, what is left unsaid;
- reflecting – reflecting back key words or phrases so that the supervisee 'hears', reflects on and clarifies meaning;
- helpful questioning – using open and hypothetical questions to encourage exploration and deep thinking on behalf of the supervisee;
- summarising – paraphrasing both the content and emotion behind what is being said in order to enable reflection and greater insight;
- challenging – encouraging supervisees to consider alternative perspectives;
- using immediacy – focusing on the 'here and now' in the supervision session;
- using silence – offering time and space for reflection;
- sharing information – considering sources of information that may be useful;
- feeding back – offering constructive criticism.

In addition, there will be new skills that come with the role – for example:

- prescribing/directing practice – informing supervisees of the law, policy or ethical issues to which they must attend.

For new supervisors it will be prescribing and directing practice that will be likely to cause the most concern or anxiety, and the skills of challenge, immediacy, feeding back and prescribing will be addressed more fully in Chapter 8. At this point, though, before supervision takes place, it is the relationship-building skills, underpinned by an empathic, authentic and non-judgemental approach, that are paramount. And, in most cases, these skills will already be firmly embedded through counselling practice.

STAGE ONE: PREPARING FOR SUPERVISION

ACTIVITY 5.4

Three supervisory relationships are introduced below, and the development of the relationship between each supervisor and supervisee will be observed over the next four chapters. Here, though, each couple is observed prior to their first meeting. As you read, make notes on the following.

1. How effectively do you feel each person is preparing for supervision with their partner?
2. Can you spot potential issues or difficulties because planning has not been carried out as effectively as it might?
3. What impact might these issues have on the effective establishment of the relationship?

Case study 5.8 Mark and Bridget

Supervisor: Mark has never supervised before. He is new to the role and is anxious that he 'gets supervision right'. Mark has been a counsellor for ten years, working as a volunteer in a couples' counselling agency for the last eight years, and it is this agency that is supporting him to make the transition to supervisor. He understands the policies and procedures of the organisation from a counsellor perspective, but, nevertheless, he arranges to see the counselling manager in order to talk through his responsibilities as a supervisor. Mark is trained as a person-centred counsellor.

  Supervisee: Bridget is a couples' counsellor with ten years' experience. She has recently moved house and has just joined Mark's organisation. Bridget has been told that she will meet her new supervisor Mark for the first time in two weeks. This is fine. Bridget has worked with six different supervisors in the past ten years and knows what she wants from supervision. Bridget is a BACP accredited counsellor with training in an integrative approach.

Case study 5.9 Fran and Gemma

Supervisor: Fran is an experienced supervisor, trained in integrative counselling and working in private practice as both a counsellor and a supervisor. Fran has been approached by the local college to work as an external supervisor for the college counselling service. Fran has agreed that counsellors visit her home, where her office is based, for supervision. Fran knows she will be supervising three counsellors, including Gemma. Fran speaks to the manager of the college counselling service on the phone. They have a brief conversation before the manager is called away, and Fran is aware that they may not have covered every detail. But she is happy to see her first supervisee, Gemma, next week.

Supervisee: Gemma is on placement at the college as a trainee counsellor. She is in year two of her integrative counselling diploma. Gemma is nervous as this is her first placement. She feels anxious about both the counselling and the supervision. Gemma has not been allocated any clients yet as the manager of the counselling service wants her to meet Fran for supervision first. Gemma has never had supervision before and is dreading it.

Case study 5.10 Karen and Clive

Supervisor: Karen has worked as a supervisor for five years for a number of voluntary agencies including a bereavement counselling service and a telephone helpline service for young people. Karen is trained in a psychodynamic counselling approach. Karen has been contacted by Clive who has recently become accredited as a counsellor and is setting up his own private counselling practice. Clive explains in an email that a friend has recommended Karen as a supervisor. Karen has not worked with a supervisee in private practice before. Clive suggests that supervision takes place at his house.

Supervisee: Clive has recently become accredited as a CBT counsellor and has decided to go into private practice. He also works as a drugs and alcohol counsellor and has made the decision to continue with his counselling at the drugs and alcohol agency where he is supervised by the agency supervisor whom he respects and values. Initially he asked his agency supervisor if she would consider supervising his private practice. She declined, but another counsellor at the agency suggested Karen as an alternative, and Clive decided to contact her to meet up.

Although it is difficult to predict how effectively the supervisory relationship will develop between each couple at this stage, there are some useful observations to be made about planning from both the supervisor and supervisee's perspective.

In the case of Mark and Bridget there are two factors that stand out as being potentially problematic. First, this is Mark's initial experience as a supervisor, and his nervousness concerning the role may be compounded by the fact that he is supervising an experienced counsellor. Second, Mark and Bridget do not share a common theoretical orientation to practice. That said, Mark has taken steps to ensure that he is prepared by arranging to meet with the agency manager to go through the organisational responsibilities of the role and to familiarise himself with the legal and policy-related issues. Furthermore, both are experienced couple counsellors and have a shared understanding of the work.

Where Fran and Gemma are concerned, both are new to working for the college, Fran as a supervisor and Gemma as a counsellor. In addition, this is Gemma's first experience of supervision, and she is anxious about what is involved. Although Fran has tried to talk through issues relating to the organisational context with the manager of the counselling service at the college, this conversation was unfortunately cut short. This may mean that there are issues concerning policy, for example, that Fran, as an external supervisor, is unclear about. There is evidence here that both supervisor and supervisee may be unprepared for supervision, for different reasons, and this may have an impact on how their relationship develops in the early stages.

The case of Karen and Clive is not straightforward either. Perhaps the most significant factor is that their theoretical orientation is not shared. Clive is a CBT counsellor and Karen is a psychodynamic-trained supervisor. This is something that Clive should have taken into account when the recommendation of Karen as a supervisor was made. There are other issues too. Karen has not supervised a counsellor in private practice before, and she should therefore reflect on what this might mean from a legal, ethical and policy perspective. She will also need to consider the issue of her fee, and it is not clear from the case study whether or not this has been discussed. Furthermore, Clive has suggested meeting at his house. Is this an initial meeting to talk about the possibility of the pair working together, or is this a first supervision session?

Chapter 6 will focus on establishing the supervisory relationship, and we will return to the three supervisory relationships above and reflect on the impact that preparation has had on the effective establishment of the relationship in each case.

CHAPTER SUMMARY

This chapter focused on the need to prepare for supervision in order that the relationship can become established and develop effectively. It examined:

- the importance of attending to a range of practicalities;
- the development of knowledge concerning the purpose and process of supervision in relation to reflective, reflexive and anti-oppressive practice, organisational, legal, policy and ethical issues, and the significance of theoretical orientation in the work;

- the transferability of counselling skills and the development of new supervisory skills in order to engage with all aspects of the role.

Where attention to the points above is paid *prior* to supervision taking place, both supervisor and supervisee are more likely to establish, develop and maintain an effective supervisory relationship.

SUGGESTED FURTHER READING

Despenser, S (2011) *What is supervision?* BACP information sheet S2. Lutterworth: BACP.

This is a useful introduction for supervisees who are new to supervision. It sets out the purpose and functions clearly in a very easily digestible form.

Scaife, J (2010) *Supervising the reflective practitioner: an essential guide to theory and practice.* London: Routledge.

A very accessible book that provides an in-depth examination of the place of reflective practice in supervision.

Wheeler, S and King, D (2001) *Supervising counsellors: issues of responsibility.* London: Sage.

A strongly recommended read that covers legal, ethical and organisational aspects of supervision practice.

CHAPTER 6

Establishing an effective supervisory relationship

Jane Westergaard

CORE KNOWLEDGE

This chapter will provide the opportunity to:

- clarify what needs to happen in the first supervision session with a new supervisor/supervisee;
- identify the key factors contributing to establishing an effective supervisory relationship;
- establish the purpose and features of a supervisory contract.

INTRODUCTION

Once preparation for a new supervisory relationship has been carried out by both supervisor and supervisee, the next step is for both parties to meet together for the first supervision session. Preparation for supervision was examined in the preceding chapter; what follows here is an exploration of the continuation of the process, whereby a relationship between a supervisor and their new supervisee can begin to be constructed.

Like any relationship, the early stages of supervision are particularly significant. If time is taken and the 'beginning' is done well, then there is every chance that a fruitful and positive relationship will ensue. If the relationship is hurried or rushed into, it may be at risk of encountering problems as it develops. Furthermore, it may be that a decision is made at this early point in the process that, for whatever reason, the supervisory relationship is not going to work and should be terminated before it develops further (Inskipp and Proctor, 1993).

This chapter begins by identifying the significance of the first meeting between supervisor and supervisee. It examines what each party should do to ensure that this meeting is both positive and productive, before exploring key factors that contribute to the effective establishment of a supervisory relationship. The chapter introduces the concept of a supervision 'contract' and details what may be contained in such a contract before considering how it is agreed. It concludes by revisiting the three supervisory relationships introduced in Chapter 5, to examine how effectively the supervisory relationship is established in each case.

THE FIRST MEETING

Meeting someone for the first time in any context can engender a range of feelings. First meetings in a professional setting can be exciting – and they can be daunting. Even where both supervisor and supervisee have prepared for their first meeting together (see Chapter 5), there is still likely to be apprehension, if not anxiety, on both sides. Regardless of how thorough each party has been in ensuring that practicalities have been attended to, that their understanding of the supervisory process is clear and that their commitment to supervision is assured, there is one thing they still do not know: how will they feel about and respond to their new supervisor/supervisee when they meet? Of course, these concerns are likely to be familiar. Most counsellors, experienced or new to the role, will face similar feelings when they embark on work with new clients. That said, there are differences between the counselling and the supervisory relationship. Although supervision contains a strong supportive, therapeutic element as well as a dynamic learning dimension, it also has a responsibility to ensure best counselling practice. Therefore, like it or not, there is an additional layer to the supervision process that is focused on making assessments about and monitoring the counsellor's work. Barden explains:

> *For the counselling profession, and for the counselled public, the supervisor remains the only person besides the client who is likely to have any consistent or detailed awareness of what goes on inside the counselling room. A duty to uphold the profession and to safeguard the public must be part of a supervisor's role, as there is currently no other place for it to be held.*
>
> (Barden, 2001, p46)

The BACP clarifies the purpose of supervision further:

- *to assist the development of the reflective practitioner;*
- *to support the therapist;*
- *to maximise the effectiveness of the therapeutic relationship;*
- *to monitor/safeguard the interests of the client;*
- *to maintain ethical standards as set out in the Ethical Framework.*

(2011, p2)

The last two bullet points emphasise the element of supervision that attends to monitoring practice and maintaining standards. It is important that both parties understand this 'normative' aspect of the process as they enter into a supervisory relationship.

ACTIVITY 6.1

Imagine that you have your very first session with a new supervisor/supervisee tomorrow. Note down a list of words that express the emotions you might be feeling.

It is likely that your list includes some or all of the following.

- Excitement.
- Fear.
- Trepidation.
- Anticipation.
- Anxiety.
- Self-doubt.
- Nervousness.
- Relief.

Even experienced supervisors and counsellors will encounter these feelings to a greater or lesser extent when they start work with a new supervisee/supervisor. If you are a supervisee who has not experienced supervision before, you are likely to feel heightened anxiety when faced with the knowledge that your counselling practice will be explored in depth. Similarly, if you are a new supervisor, you may be experiencing corresponding anxieties about offering 'good enough' supervision to your supervisee. It is helpful to reflect that a new counselling client might well write a similar list of their feelings before attending their first counselling session. This demonstrates one of the ways in which supervision mirrors the counselling process.

The purpose of the first supervision meeting, like the first counselling session (that parallel process again), is to provide a forum where honest and open communication can take place. The building of a trusting relationship can begin, whereby the supervisor offers a 'safe space' in which thoughts, feelings and actions can be contained, addressed and managed effectively.

There is, however, an activity that should be managed in the first supervision session, as it is central to the effective establishment of the supervisory relationship but is nevertheless a discrete element of the process. This is the agreement of a supervisory 'contract' between supervisor, supervisee and, possibly, the counselling agency or organisation for which the counsellor works. We will examine the features of this contract later in the chapter. First, let us consider what needs to happen in this first meeting in order that the early stages of the supervisory relationship are managed effectively.

ACTIVITY 6.2

If you are a new supervisor, reflect on the very first supervision session that you had as a supervisee. Ask yourself what elements were addressed in that first session? What worked well? What did your supervisor say or do that was helpful? If you are new to supervision, take a moment to think about what you would *like* to be covered in the first session. What kind of things might be discussed that would help you to feel comfortable to engage in the process? What kind of approach would you like your supervisor to take with you?

Inskipp and Proctor (2009) suggest that the first meeting should ask (and answer) a key question: whether or not both parties can engage effectively in the supervision process. This should be done by exploring what supervision means to each participant (supervisor and supervisee) and by sharing thoughts, hopes, fears, beliefs and values concerning counselling and supervision. McMahon concurs but places an emphasis on the need to clarify the practical elements of supervision. She suggests a list of sample questions that could inform a first meeting.

- *When will we meet, for how long and where?*
- *What costs are involved and how is payment preferred?*
- *What happens if one of us wants to cancel our meeting?*
- *How available is the supervisor between sessions for the supervisee if he/she experiences difficulties?*
- *What records will be kept of our supervision, where will they be kept and by whom?*
- *What is expected of the supervisee in presenting cases and issues for supervision, for example does he/she bring detailed case notes or a video recording?*
- *What reporting, if any, will occur, what process will it follow, and who will receive copies?*
- *How will confidentiality and other issues be dealt with?*

(2002, p21)

This is an interesting and, perhaps, surprising list of questions that, as suggested, focus more on clarifying the practical elements of the relationship than on defining the expectations and understanding of the supervision process. But being clear about the practicalities involved in the process (as discussed in Chapter 5) is central to being able to engage confidently in a trusting relationship. A first session that does not address issues of confidentiality, boundaries, payment, attendance, record keeping and so on has failed in its responsibility to promote an open and transparent process. The list above should not be seen as prescriptive, and it is important that the practicalities alone do not constitute the content of a first supervisory session. Below are some additional points to be discussed with someone new to supervision.

- What is our shared understanding of the supervision process?
- Who is supervision for?
- What do we want to achieve?
- What are our hopes and fears concerning the process?
- What will a 'typical' supervision session involve?
- What is the role of the supervisor? And the supervisee?
- How should we prepare before each session?
- What theoretical orientation underpins our practice?

It is, perhaps, these questions that will form the larger part of the discussion in the first session. And it is important that supervision, even at a first meeting where practicalities are established, maintains a *dialogue* between supervisor and supervisee. McMahon's questions, set out above, suggest a wealth of information sharing on the part of the supervisor. This is all useful and necessary stuff, but the effect of providing this information could be that it is the voice of the supervisor that dominates and the supervisee does not feel engaged in the process. To reduce this risk, it might be helpful to begin the session by focusing on questions concerning the *process* of supervision and the *expectations* of both parties, before moving on later in the interaction to consider the *practicalities*.

ACTIVITY 6.3

Below are two examples of an opening exchange in a first supervision session with a new supervisee. What are your thoughts about how effectively each is managed?

Example one

Supervisor: *Hello, Carly. Good to meet you at last. As you know I'm Steve, your supervisor, here at your counselling placement. I understand that this is your first experience of supervision?*

Supervisee: *Um . . . yes . . . yes, it is.*

Supervisor: *OK . . . well, welcome! It's good to meet you. I'm looking forward to us starting to work together, and I'm wondering how you're feeling about this first session?*

Supervisee: *Um . . . I don't know really . . . a bit strange, I guess . . . a bit anxious, to be honest. I'm not really sure what this is all about. I mean I've got a vague idea, you know, from my tutors at college, but um . . .*

Supervisor: *Yes, well, as you say, any new experience can be strange . . . and I guess supervision is no exception. But it's good that you have, as you express it, a 'vague idea' about what's involved. Would it help if we spent some time now trying to get to grips in more detail with what supervision is all about? Later on we can look at some of the practicalities of these sessions too. It's important that we're both clear about our responsibilities. But first, how about having a go at making your 'vague idea' a bit clearer and thinking about what supervision for counsellors actually means?*

Supervisee: *Um . . . yeah . . . I mean, well, yes, I think that would help. Definitely.*

Supervisor: *Good. OK, then, why don't we start with a conversation that shares our thoughts about the process. Can we begin with what you think supervision is all about?*

Example two

Supervisor: *Hi! It's Dave, isn't it?*

Supervisee: *Yes, that's right.*

Supervisor: *Great. Well I'm Ian, and I'm your supervisor. And this is the first time we've met isn't it?*

Supervisee: *Yes . . . yes it is.*

Supervisor: *And I'm aware that you haven't had supervision before? You're new to all this?*

Supervisee: *Er, no. No, I haven't. This is my first time.*

Supervisor: *Good. Well . . . I guess we need to start by making sure that we are clear about our responsibilities as supervisor and supervisee. We also need to agree a contract for supervision, and we'll get that done a bit later in this session. But before any of that, let me tell you something about counselling supervision and my experience as a supervisor. OK? Would that be useful?*

Both examples begin by focusing on the process rather than the practicalities of supervision. This is good. But example two suggests that it is the supervisor's role to *tell* the supervisee what supervision is all about rather than to engage in a *conversation* about its purpose and functions. The danger here is that a climate of 'I'm the expert' may unwittingly ensue. This could harm the development of a mutually open, trusting and respectful relationship where it is the *supervisee and their practice* that forms the focus of supervision. In example one, the supervisor invites the supervisee to share her understanding of what supervision is all about. The sub-text here is that the supervisee's knowledge and views are central to the discussions that take place in supervision and will be encouraged and valued from the outset.

There is one important point that should not be overlooked at this stage. Inskipp and Proctor suggest that the aim of the first meeting is to reach a conclusion about whether or not the supervisee and supervisor can work together. This is certainly true in private practice where the counsellor and supervisor have a strong element of choice concerning who they work with. But in many organisations there is limited or no choice about these supervision arrangements. Where this is the case, it is even more important that the early stages of the supervision relationship are managed effectively. Mearns summarises:

> *Whatever the supervision context, however, experience has shown me that my most important task is to establish the kind of relationship which makes possible the freedom and non-defensiveness desired.*
>
> (Mearns, 1991, p116)

WHAT MAKES A 'GOOD' RELATIONSHIP?

Weaks (2002) examines the features of 'good supervision', and, perhaps unsurprisingly, the factors that are identified as being central to effective supervisory relationships mirror those that are valued by clients in counselling. In particular, it is the quality of the relationship, built on a genuine, empathic and non-judgemental approach that is cited as central. It is important to stress that this book does not promote a particular theoretical orientation to supervision (although both authors subscribe to an integrative approach to counselling). However, evidence suggests that many counsellors and supervisors concur, regardless of their training, that it is the core conditions of person-centred practice that underpin their work (Westergaard, 2012). It is therefore worth taking a moment to review these core conditions (Rogers, 1951) and consider their applicability to the supervision context.

REFLECTION POINT

Take some time to reflect on your own approach to counselling clients (or, if you have not yet started counselling, what your training has taught you about what is needed to establish a positive relationship between client and counsellor). Note down the factors that you think are most important in ensuring an effective working relationship. Now reflect on how far these factors might be applied to a supervisory relationship too.

In Case study 6.1 to what extent does Carrie, a counsellor and supervisor, echo your thoughts?

Case study 6.1 Carrie: counsellor

I've been a counsellor, working in mental health and other settings, and a supervisor of mental health counsellors for some time. It never ceases to amaze me how the approach I take in my work with clients mirrors what I offer in supervision. The contexts and content of sessions differ, but the core conditions apply to both. What I mean is that I try to offer empathy, congruence and unconditional positive regard both to clients and to supervisees. This means working hard to understand what my clients and supervisees are going through, to be genuine and real in the relationship with each and to try not to make judgements; or at least to 'manage' the judgements I know I am making. It is this acceptance and valuing of both clients and supervisees, I believe, that leads to the development of a trusting relationship. It's not easy and it takes time, but without knowing about and adhering to the core conditions, I think that most of these relationships could be at risk and, probably in many cases, would fail.

Carrie is clear in her assertion that it is the core conditions of empathy, congruence and unconditional positive regard (UPR) that underpin and sustain both her counselling and supervisory relationships. Mearns (1991) suggests four basic conditions that are central to supervision practice:

- *commitment;*
- *congruence;*
- *valuing;*
- *empathy.*

It is not difficult to discern the core conditions of person-centred practice in this list (congruence, valuing (UPR) and empathy). In addition, the concept of 'commitment' is introduced. Mearns explains that commitment means engaging with, and investing in, every aspect of the supervisory relationship – including the challenging or problematic elements that may develop. Commitment is about being professional and means taking the relationship and the supervisee seriously.

The principles of person-centred practice are embedded in the importance of the 'here and now' (Mearns and Thorne, 2007; Prever, 2010). Transposed to the supervision context, this suggests that the supervisor should not only be attending to *what* the supervisee is saying but also to *how* they are presenting. This requires highly developed reflexive skills on the part of the supervisor. As with clients, it is very easy to become embroiled in the 'story' and lose sight of what is really happening 'in the moment'. Furthermore, attendance to the developing relationship should uncover potential issues of power or oppressive practice. Paying explicit attention to developing anti-oppressive practice is vital at this early stage (see Chapters 2 and 5) in order that 'difference' can be acknowledged and explored openly.

Case study 6.2 Core conditions in practice in a first supervision session

Supervisor: *Can we just pause for a moment? You've explained about where you are in your counsellor training, and I know that you are using a cognitive behavioural approach in your work with clients. It's interesting, though, that as you're talking I'm sensing a hesitation . . . I don't know . . . maybe a hesitation, maybe a reluctance to talk about the approach you use. Maybe something else altogether. Have I got that 'hesitation' right?*

Supervisee: *No . . . no, I don't think so. Well, I mean obviously it's very early days. You know I've only just started seeing clients, and this is my first experience of supervision. Maybe I am a bit hesitant, a bit reluctant . . . I don't know . . . maybe I have been holding back a bit.*

Supervisor: *Yes, 'holding back', that's a good way to describe what I've been sensing has been happening in this session. And what do you think the 'holding back' might be about?*

Supervisee: *Um . . . I don't know really. I suppose it could be a few things.*

Supervisor: *Yes, absolutely, I guess so. What kind of things? Any ideas?*

Supervisee: *Well . . . I could be feeling a bit insecure. I mean, this is all very new to me, this . . . this, well, counselling. Yes, I've been trained, but actually putting my training into practice is another thing altogether. And maybe, maybe, it's about this relationship too. You know. You and me. Maybe I'm worried that you'll think I'm doing it all wrong, that I'm not good enough. That I'm messing up. I don't know . . . I mean you've been doing this for a while and you're really experienced . . . .*

Supervisor: *They sound like very good reasons why someone might 'hold back' when they first come to supervision. And it strikes me too that clients might feel the same way when they come to their first counselling session. And on top of that I might be feeling that way too, with a new supervisee. What do you think?*

Supervisee: *Yes, I guess so . . . I suppose clients might feel a bit intimidated by it all . . .*

Supervisor: *So what would you say to a new client who seems to be holding back in the early days of counselling?*

Supervisee: *Um . . . I don't know really. I guess I might say that this is a safe space and that we can take time to explore things and work together . . . and that they are not being judged or criticised. That kind of thing, I suppose . . .*

Supervisor: *Wonderful! And do you know what? That is exactly what I want to say to you. That this is a safe place, where you won't be judged and we can work together . . . but I know it's not only about saying the words. I've got to show you that I'm OK. And it's going to take time for you to trust this relationship with me, just like it does for your clients to trust their relationships with you. And yes, I might be experienced in supervision, but I too might have anxieties about being a 'good enough' supervisor for you. So what do you think we can do here to help you to feel safe enough to open up rather than 'hold back'?*

In this example, the supervisor invites the supervisee to stay in the 'here and now' and focus on the relationship developing between them. The supervisor also makes the link between supervision and the counselling process. This is helpful as it enables the supervisee to reflect on the parallel relationship with clients. The core conditions are evident as the supervisor is empathic, genuine and 'real', using immediacy in the relationship, and not making judgements about how her supervisee is presenting. As the supervisor in this example suggests, the relationship will take time to build. But by discussing this at the outset and adhering to person-centred core conditions throughout, a climate is generated in which, it is hoped, the relationship will thrive.

In the same way that the counsellor in the example above is new to supervision and demonstrating some anxiety about the process, a new supervisor may also have concerns. Whether or not to disclose that this is a first experience of supervision is something that each individual supervisor should reflect on before they meet their supervisee for the first time. It might help to consider *why* a supervisee might need this information or find it useful and *how* it might be shared. Again, attendance to the parallel process could be helpful here. Would counsellors expect to share with their clients that this is their first experience of counselling, and if so, how would they do it? There is no right or wrong approach concerning whether or not the supervisor chooses to discuss their inexperience. It is essential, though, that the decision is informed by person-centred principles, whereby it is the needs of the *supervisee* that are paramount.

In addition to embracing the core conditions of person-centred practice, Hawkins and Shohet (2006) develop a list of qualities for supervisors. The list includes:

- flexibility in approach;
- seeing a situation from a range of perspectives;
- a sound understanding of the discipline/context in which they supervise;
- adherence to a multicultural approach;
- an ability to contain anxiety – their own and their supervisee's;
- a positive approach to learning;
- being sensitive to the wider context;
- managing the power dynamic;
- a sense of humour, patience and humility.

The points above will be attended to as we follow the development of the supervisory relationship in subsequent chapters. But it is helpful to be aware of these elements at the outset.

REFLECTION POINT

If you are a new supervisor, consider each element outlined in the list above. Which of these features do you feel confident about? Which are you unsure of? Which do you feel you need to develop? If you are a new counsellor, how does this list differ from what is required in counselling relationships with clients?

With one or two exceptions, the list could equally be applied to the relationship between counsellor and client. Adhering to this list from the outset requires the following.

- Flexibility in approach: discussing the practicalities of supervision with the supervisee to ensure that both parties are comfortable with where, when, how often and so on, supervision will take place.

- Seeing a situation from a range of perspectives: encouraging the discussion of clients and counselling-related issues and problems; helping supervisees to conceptualise, explore and examine their practice in new ways; illuminating client work and contributing to the supervisee's knowledge and development.

- A sound understanding of the discipline/context in which they supervise: helping the supervisee to articulate the issues clients raise, which relate to their counselling context (for example, addiction, bereavement, youth counselling, and so on); using their own knowledge of the context to share ideas, theories and developments to inform the supervisee's practice.

- A multicultural approach: being explicit about and discussing cultural factors in both counselling practice and the supervisory relationship; developing a shared understanding of anti-oppressive practice and of multicultural working.

- An ability to contain anxiety – their own and their supervisees: building a relationship based on trust whereby supervisees feel able to share the complexities, anxieties and challenges of their practice; ensuring that they make use of their own supervision to 'manage' their own feelings relating to the supervisory role.

- A positive approach to learning: responding to different perspectives and new knowledge shared by supervisees in a positive way; recognising that there is learning to be gained by the supervisor too; sharing knowledge and encouraging engagement with new knowledge through reading, training and so on.

- Being sensitive to the wider context: gaining an understanding of the supervisee from both a professional and personal context; engaging with the 'whole' person.

- Managing the power dynamic: first, recognising that however hard the supervisor tries to engender a relationship based on equality, there is a power dynamic at play. It relates to the normative function of supervision whereby 'monitoring' of practice is the responsibility of the supervisor. However, that is not the same as suggesting that the supervisor is 'the expert' holding all the answers.

- A sense of humour, patience and humility: this relates to the core condition of congruence. It means being real in the relationship, encouraging curiosity and playfulness in the work, taking time to 'discover' rather than 'instruct' and includes admitting mistakes.

There is much that both supervisor and supervisee can do to ensure that the supervisory relationship has the best start. The first meeting should be carefully constructed, and the supervisee must feel involved in the process from the outset – even when there are practicalities to be discussed. Furthermore, the supervisor should adhere to the core conditions in order that a respectful climate is provided in which a relationship of openness and trust develops. Finally, the supervisor should reflect on the points outlined above, reminding themselves of the importance of such factors as context, power and cultural issues as they engage with their supervisee for the first time.

There is one significant activity that should take place in the first supervision session and that has not been discussed in detail thus far: contracting. The agreement of a contract ensures that at the end of the first supervision session the supervisor, the supervisee and, where appropriate, the counselling organisation or agency are clear about their responsibilities and rights.

CONTRACTING

Much has been written about contracting in supervision (Hewson, 1999; Barden, 2001; Page and Wosket, 2001; Hawkins and Shohet, 2006). What follows seeks to distil the key elements of the contracting process and reflect on why and how contracting takes place. Barden explains:

> *Contracting is an agreement between two parties, of lawful object, of mutual benefit undertaken on both sides. This is the overt process. Alongside this are all kinds of covert contracts and these, if not brought into conscious awareness from time to time, affect both psychotherapy process, counselling, management and supervision.*
>
> (Barden, 2001, p69)

The reference to overt and covert processes in contracting here is helpful. It is to reduce the risk of covert contracts that the process should be as open and rigorous as possible. In particular, time should be taken in the first session to clarify exactly what contracting means. Contracting sounds like a formal process, and in many ways it is. But the true purpose of a supervision contract is to provide protection and support rather than indicate a constrained or potentially punitive process.

ACTIVITY 6.4

Take a moment to note down the reasons for contracting in supervision. It might help to reflect on the contracting process in counselling first. Why might counsellors agree contracts with their clients? Why might contracting be equally important in supervision?

Hawkins and Shohet (2006) explain the importance of contracting in order to protect and support supervisors, supervisees and clients. They suggest six areas that should be covered by a supervision contract.

- Practicalities – for example, arrangements for meeting.

- Boundaries – making clear the distinction between therapy, management and supervision, and setting out the limits of confidentiality.

- Working alliance – a shared understanding of what constitutes supervision, what style of supervision is needed and how it will be delivered.

- The session format – what a typical session might look like.

- The organisational and professional context – the organisation's policy on supervision (if appropriate), the professional code of conduct and statement of ethics that applies.

- Taking notes – how notes are taken, how they are recorded, who has access to them and where they are kept.

Hawkins and Shohet are at pains to point out that every aspect of the contract should be discussed fully before agreement is reached. This will ensure that both supervisor and supervisee are clear about what is required. Barden concurs, stating that transparent contracting:

creates a negotiated and mutually respectful supervisory relationship where tasks, functions and responsibilities are understood by both parties and where the professional development of the supervisee is paramount and the care and protection of clients is assured.

(Barden, 2001, p82)

Despenser (2009) provides an example of a supervision contract that offers a useful starting point. And the concept of a contract as a 'starting point' is important. All contracts should be reviewed after a period of time has elapsed, once supervisor and supervisee have had the opportunity to reflect on how their supervisory relationship is progressing.

The testimony below demonstrates the need for contracting in supervision.

Case study 6.3 Jermaine: supervisee

I've had two quite different experiences of contracting in supervision. The first was when I was on placement as a school counsellor, and the second was when I started work as a counsellor in a youth agency. In the school setting, I actually met my supervisor for the first time before I'd started counselling. She asked me what I thought supervision was all about, and she let me know about how and when supervision would happen, you know, the practical details. She brought along a prepared contract pro-forma with her and went through it with me in detail. This really helped me to understand what supervision was all about and what my rights and responsibilities were.

In the second experience, I'd already started counselling before I had supervision, and when I met my supervisor for the first time we talked straight away about my counselling, as I was struggling with a particularly challenging client. At the end of the session I asked my supervisor about record keeping and confidentiality and stuff like that. To be honest . . . he didn't seem very sure. He said that he'd go away and find out and get back to me. But this was after I'd already talked about some difficult personal issues that I was experiencing. This left me feeling a bit twitchy.

Jermaine highlights the importance of contracting in the early stages of supervision. His first supervisor came prepared with a written contract that was subsequently discussed and agreed, and Jermaine found this useful. Written contracts might be helpful, and it is worthwhile checking with your organisation (if you are working for an organisation) about what form of contract exists. If you are supervising privately, you may want to consider developing your own pro-forma – not to be introduced as a prescription for supervision but more as a 'living' document that can be adapted and amended as appropriate. Where Jermaine's second supervisor appeared unsure about issues such as record keeping, Jermaine was left experiencing anxiety – not a good start for building a trusting and respectful supervisory relationship.

So far in this chapter we have looked at the elements that contribute to establishing an effective supervisory relationship. These include:

- paying attention to the content of the first session and clarifying areas for discussion;

- adhering to the core conditions in order to establish an open and trusting relationship;

- identifying potential issues of oppressive practice and responding appropriately;

- completing a contracting process whereby both parties are clear about rights, responsibilities, boundaries and ethical working.

STAGE TWO: ESTABLISHING AN EFFECTIVE SUPERVISORY RELATIONSHIP

ACTIVITY 6.5

Let us now return to the three supervisory relationships introduced in Chapter 5. Here we met Mark and Bridget, Fran and Gemma, and Karen and Clive – three supervisors and their new supervisees. In Chapter 5 we considered how effectively each had prepared for supervision. The first supervision session has now taken place. As you read about their first sessions (below), make notes on the following.

1. How effectively is the relationship established?
2. What is done well?
3. What, if anything, is missing from the first session?

Case study 6.4 Mark and Bridget

As Mark is new to supervising he is, not surprisingly, feeling nervous during this first session with experienced couple counsellor Bridget. He finds himself talking too much and 'telling' Bridget what supervision is all about. Bridget gently reminds Mark that she has had six previous supervisors and is familiar with what the process involves. Mark takes a deep breath, slows down and asks Bridget what she wants and needs from supervision. This helps a dialogue to develop. Bridget explains that she works integratively, and Mark responds openly concerning his own person-centred theoretical orientation. Both agree that the difference in approach does not necessarily constitute a problem, particularly as they are both experienced counsellors working in the same context: couple counselling. They agree to monitor this as supervision proceeds. It is only once the session ends and Mark breathes a sigh of relief, that he realises he hasn't agreed an explicit contract for supervision with Bridget. They have discussed a number of practicalities, but there is nothing in writing and the contract pro-forma his manager gave him to complete in the session is still in his pocket. He is unsure what to do now. He reaches for the phone to dial Bridget's number and then thinks better of it. Mark makes a call instead to the counselling manager at the couple counselling agency to ask her advice.

Case study 6.5 Fran and Gemma

Fran, an experienced supervisor working in private practice, has agreed to be an external supervisor for Gemma, a trainee counsellor on her first placement at a local college. Gemma arrives late for her first supervision as she can't find Fran's house, where the supervision is to take place. This means that Gemma is flustered, as well as nervous, as the session begins. Fran asks her what she thinks supervision is all about. Gemma is unsure. She feels intimidated and anxious about saying the 'wrong thing' to Fran as she's so new to the process. Fran asks Gemma about her counselling practice so far, and Gemma explains that she hasn't seen any clients yet as her manager wanted her to meet with Fran first. Fran is unaware of this arrangement and feels awkward for having asked the question about client work when it is not relevant. Fran goes on to suggest that they spend the time focusing on Gemma's feelings about starting work with clients. Gemma relaxes and agrees that this will be useful. Gemma also asks Fran not to tell her line manager how anxious she is feeling about counselling. Fran agrees, but she is aware that she has not yet had a detailed conversation with Gemma's manager about issues such as boundaries and confidentiality. Gemma asks if anything she says in supervision will be written down or recorded. Again, Fran is unsure. She explains that she will speak to Gemma's manager at the college before the next supervision session to gain clarification on these points, and she suggests that they agree a supervisory contract together next time they meet.

Case study 6.6 Karen and Clive

Karen meets her supervisee, Clive, at his house. Clive explains that he is setting out in private practice as a CBT counsellor and this is why he needs a supervisor. He reminds Karen that he also works as a drugs and alcohol counsellor at an agency where he is supervised by the agency supervisor. Karen shares her experience as a supervisor and explains that she hasn't supervised a counsellor working in private practice before – although she is looking forward to it. Karen has brought with her the contract that she uses at the counselling agency where she currently supervises volunteer counsellors. She suggests that they use this as a starting point for developing their own contract. Karen has also brought a BACP information sheet on supervision and suggests that they work through it together. Clive feels a little frustrated as he is hoping to talk about a client with whom he is struggling. He explains that he does not recall going through a similar process when he first had supervision at the agency. Karen is aware of Clive's impatience to get on and at the same time she begins to feel that perhaps she is being unnecessarily cautious. She invites Clive to talk about the contracting process he goes through with his new, private clients. Clive asks how this is relevant. He is starting to think that he's made a mistake with Karen. She seems more focused on filling in a form than she does on talking about his clients. After 30 minutes Clive voices his concerns that perhaps this relationship isn't working. Karen suggests that they take some time to explore the role of contracting in supervision and the significance of contracting in private practice with clients. She hopes that by drawing a parallel between counselling and supervision, Clive will see the importance of the contracting process. Together they consider some hypothetical situations that could arise, both with counselling clients and in supervision. Clive engages with the discussion and suggests that he had not, perhaps, given issues such as confidentiality and boundaries enough thought. As Karen drives away, she realises that they have not discussed the question of her fee and she has come away without being paid for her time.

Each of the three supervisory relationships detailed above show that there is no such thing as a perfect first session. This is helpful. In a book such as this there is a risk that the process may seem mechanistic, and the human element, which is as central to supervision as it is to counselling, can appear to be overlooked. In all three examples the first session is approached in a different way, but in each case there is evidence that a relationship is establishing.

Mark and Bridget seem to have got off to a fine start, sharing their experiences of supervision and spending time discussing the fact that they practise using different counselling approaches. A dialogue such as this is healthy and demonstrates an early level of trust and openness. The fact that Mark has neglected to complete a formal written contract with Bridget might be problematic. But key practical issues have been discussed, and Mark has acted appropriately by seeking advice from the counselling manager at the agency.

Fran and Gemma have also navigated the first session effectively. Clearly, it would have helped if Fran had managed to have a full discussion with Gemma's manager at her counselling placement at the college *before* she and Gemma met for the first time. It was only during the first session that a number of questions and issues arose for Fran, as an external supervisor, that she realised would require answers before the next session. However, Fran was able to contain Gemma's anxiety about counselling, and they began to build a trusting relationship together. Evidently Gemma felt safe enough to share her concerns with her supervisor. Although Fran was left feeling that she was underprepared for the session, Gemma reflected on how useful it had been to talk openly with someone about her fears and anxieties.

In the case of Karen and Clive, the first supervision meeting was challenging. First, the meeting took place at Clive's house. Although there is nothing to stop this happening, it might raise issues concerned with safe working and oppressive practice. Both parties therefore must be mindful of this and feel comfortable with the arrangement. Although Karen had prepared fully, had thought about a supervision contract and had taken the BACP supervision guidelines with her to the first session, Clive was keen to get on and talk about client work. At one stage it appeared as though the relationship might falter before it began. But with Karen's careful persistence and Clive's gradual realisation concerning the importance of contracting, they were able to establish a dialogue and work through their different perspectives. As yet, the concept of theoretical orientation (Karen is a psychodynamic practitioner whereas Clive is trained in a CBT approach) has not been discussed. Furthermore, Karen must reflect on why it was that the issue of her payment was overlooked, and she must consider what action she needs to take to rectify this.

In the next chapter we will explore stage three of the supervisory relationship model: progressing the supervisory relationship. We will revisit Mark and Bridget, Fran and Gemma, and Karen and Clive to see how effectively they are working together after a number of supervision sessions.

CHAPTER SUMMARY

This chapter explored the factors that impact on establishing a supervisory relationship effectively. It examined:

- the features of the first session and what needs to happen in the first meeting between supervisor and supervisee to ensure that the relationship gets off to a positive start;

- the factors that constitute an effective supervisory relationship, including the core conditions of a person-centred approach alongside an awareness of managing the power dynamic;

- the importance of contracting in supervision to ensure that a working agreement between both parties (and the counselling agency or organisation) is in place.

By taking the time to ensure that these factors are addressed early on, the relationship between supervisor and supervisee should be grounded in trust and openness from the outset. As it progresses, building on these foundations, a sound working alliance has the best opportunity to develop.

SUGGESTED FURTHER READING

Hawkins, P and Shohet, R (2006) *Supervision in the helping professions,* 3rd edition. Milton Keynes: Open University Press.

Chapter 6, in particular, explores the building of the supervisory relationship, including issues of contracting.

Holloway, E and Carroll, M (eds) (1999) *Training counselling supervisors.* London: Sage.

Although a little dated, this text includes an excellent chapter on contracting in supervision (Chapter 3).

Inskipp, F and Proctor, B (2009) *Making the most of supervision,* 2nd edition. Twickenham: Cascade.

An excellent read, accessible and well informed. Useful for both supervisors and supervisees new to the process.

CHAPTER 7

Progressing the supervisory relationship

Jane Westergaard

CORE KNOWLEDGE

This chapter will provide the opportunity to:

- examine key theories and concepts relating to the development of an effective supervisory relationship;
- clarify the terms 'transference' and 'counter-transference';
- identify the key principles of transactional analysis as a means to

---

INTRODUCTION

So far we have looked at stages one and two of a five-stage model that charts the development of the supervisory relationship: stage one focuses on 'preparing' for supervision and stage two goes on to emphasise the 'establishment' stage of the relationship. In this chapter, we continue our exploration of the developing relationship between supervisee and supervisor by considering the factors that influence its progression. Where thorough preparation prior to supervision taking place is paramount (stage one) and the first encounter between both parties establishes the foundations on which the relationship is built (stage two), it is stage three, where supervisor and supervisee begin to develop their relationship and engage with the work in-depth, that is perhaps the most critical.

The chapter begins with a review of key developmental theories relating to supervision, introduced in Chapter 3, and examines how these theories can be applied in supervision practice. It makes reference to the concept of transference and counter-transference, mentioned already in this book. In particular, it begins to examine how the relationship between supervisor and supervisee should move towards developing an 'internal supervisor', a voice that becomes increasingly present 'within' the supervisee. Finally, this chapter introduces the concept of transactional analysis as a means to understand and develop open and effective communication between supervisor and supervisee (paralleling what happens between counsellor and client). At the end of the chapter we will return to our three supervisory relationships to examine how effectively each relationship is progressing.

DEVELOPMENTAL THEORIES

Interestingly, theories of development relating specifically to the activity of supervision rather than counselling do exist (Stoltenberg, 1981; Stoltenberg and Delworth, 1987; Holloway, 1995; Stoltenberg et al. 1998; Shulman, 2006; Hawkins and Shohet, 2006), but the word 'development' is in itself problematic. For example, some of these 'developmental' models chart the progress of the *relationship* between supervisor and supervisee (Shulman, 2006), while others examine the development of the *supervisee* through the process of supervision (Stoltenberg et al., 1998). Hawkins and Shohet's model examines the development of the supervision *process*, suggesting key characteristics required for supervision to fulfil its purpose and progress effectively. Carroll raises some important issues regarding developmental models, particularly those that focus on the development of the supervisee. He asserts that:

> *Developmental models do not indicate how change takes place but merely state the stages through which supervisees move. How are such models connected to supervisors, to the supervisory relationship, to the personality of the supervisee? All these are unanswered questions within the supervisory literature.*

> (Carroll, 1996, p16)

Although Carroll voiced his concerns in 1996, little research to address his questions appears to have taken place since. That is not to say that knowledge of developmental models is unhelpful or that new models have ceased to emerge. In fact, in my experience of training supervisors, students have found it helpful to gain an understanding of the developments taking place in supervision from a range of perspectives: the *supervisory relationship*, the *supervisee* and the *process of supervision*.

We already know there are models that chart the development of the supervisory relationship, and Chapters 5 to 9 of this book are devoted to navigating its development, making reference to a five-stage process identified below.

- Preparing.
- Establishing.
- Progressing.
- Working alliance.
- Ending.

At this point, when focusing on how the *relationship* enters its 'progression' phase, it is helpful to consider other developments that are taking place. So, what follows here builds on our knowledge of concepts introduced in Chapter 3, including Stoltenberg et al.'s developmental model, examining the development of the *supervisee* through supervision, and Hawkins and Shohet's process model, focusing on the supervision *process*.

Stoltenberg et al.'s developmental model

Hawkins and Shohet (2006) offer a useful summary of a range of developmental models, including Stoltenberg and Delworth's (1987), which they describe as incorporating four levels of development. These levels are detailed in Chapter 3.

Stoltenberg et al. (1998) went on to propose an integrated development model (IDM), emphasising the warmth, understanding, trust, respect and acceptance that underpins the effective development of any helping relationship, while also describing different stages or 'levels' of supervisee development within the supervision process. The IDM model identifies three levels of supervisees' development outlined below.

- *Level one* This level is characterised by the supervisee's feelings of anxiety. The supervisee is new to supervision, keen to do well, but uncertain about what supervision involves. At this stage the supervisee is seeking guidance and reassurance, anxious to draw on their supervisor's knowledge, expertise and experience, suggesting high levels of dependency in the relationship. Although this level of development is particularly apparent in supervisees who are new to the process, even experienced supervisees are likely to recognise some of the feelings engendered at level one when they begin work with a new supervisor.

- *Level two* If level one is successfully negotiated, supervisees should begin to understand the process of supervision and develop deeper reflective and reflexive skills. That is not to say they are entirely confident in their practice. Indeed, confidence at this stage is fragile and can be shattered easily if supervisees perceive a lack of progress in the work. This level has been compared to adolescence, whereby the supervisee is experiencing feelings of independence (and even omnipotence) one moment, and inadequacy and dependency the next. The risk here is that supervisees become so immersed in their clients' worlds that issues of transference and counter-transference prevail, often resulting in a loss of direction and feelings of 'stuckness'.

- *Level three* Supervisees who reach level three will have overcome the challenges of level two. The 'internal supervisor' is beginning to emerge, so supervisees can remain empathic to their clients while reflecting objectively on the work and developing greater reflexivity. This level is characterised by the supervisee demonstrating skills of 'self-supervision', using sessions effectively with little dependence on the supervisor.

REFLECTION POINT

Reflect on your own history of supervision, as a supervisee, not a supervisor. Can you identify the level you have reached in your current supervision? What did your supervisor do that enabled you to progress from one level to the next? If you are yet to receive supervision, it is likely that you can relate to some of the feelings detailed in level one. If this is the case, how might your supervisor help you through this phase?

Theo is an experienced supervisor working with several supervisees. In Case study 7.1 she identifies three supervisees who she feels provide good examples of each level of development.

Case study 7.1 Theo: supervisor

Level one: *I have seen Sian for three supervision sessions. I think we are making progress, but she is definitely still very anxious about the whole process. I find myself feeling responsible for her, parental almost. I guess that this is the transference operating. Sian is wanting and needing me to look after her and make her feel OK, just like 'mummy' would, and I'm trying to resist the very strong desire to play 'mummy' and rescue or infantilise her.*

Level two: *Jonah worked through the dependency level quickly. He is much more 'secure' in his work than he was initially, but I've discovered that his confidence can be shaken very easily and replaced by self-doubt. He feels responsible for his clients rather than to them, and this leads to a tendency to become over-involved and not be able to separate himself from the work. Sometimes I want to ask Jonah what he thinks will happen to his clients if he ceases to exist. I feel that he needs to develop a perspective concerning where he 'fits' as a counsellor. He is not there to solve clients' problems or manage their lives. It's all about becoming a more reflexive counsellor. We're getting there, I think.*

Level three: *Vrinda is an experienced counsellor and we have been working together in supervision for a long while. I intervene very little in sessions; I ask Vrinda what she wants to talk about . . . and off she goes. Her reflections are always insightful and she*

> is both thoughtful and curious about her work. Vrinda has developed a strong sense of self in relation to others and has a powerful awareness of her own responses and intuitions. She can still be hard on herself – self-critical – but her 'internal supervisor' is ever-present. I'd describe our relationship as collaborative, two professional people working together.

Theo describes her work with three supervisees who are at different stages in their development. Sian, at level one, is feeling anxious and is looking to Theo for answers. Jonah, at level two, has progressed beyond dependency on Theo, but is finding it difficult to remain 'separate' from the work, and Vrinda, at level three, is exhibiting high levels of autonomy, using well-developed reflective and reflexive skills to examine her practice. In a moment we will consider how Theo might work with Sian, Jonah and Vrinda to help them to continue to develop in supervision but, first, we need to remind ourselves about the important concepts of transference and counter-transference, which have been alluded to in this chapter (and previously in Chapter 3) and which counsellors will have been introduced to – along with other theories and concepts underpinning psychodynamic approaches to counselling – in their training.

As explained earlier, transference refers to a way of understanding how our past experiences and relationships can, unconsciously, become significant in the present (Embleton, 2002). For example, we may come into contact with someone who arouses feelings in us that we have experienced in a previous relationship in our lives. We are likely to respond unconsciously to the 'current' acquaintance in the same way that we did to the person in the original relationship – this is transference. The counter-transference comes when the new acquaintance finds themselves responding to our unconscious transference rather than to the reality of the here and now.

For example, I recall experiencing deep affection and warmth on meeting my first supervisor. In return, it seemed, my supervisor responded to me by taking care of me. I felt very safe in the relationship, almost protected. As the relationship developed, we discussed these feelings. My supervisor had become aware that the impetus to shelter and protect me was perhaps inhibiting my development as a counsellor – and also uncharacteristic of the way she normally worked with supervisees. During one session she asked me the question: *Who am I to you?* This disconcerted me to begin with, but as I reflected more deeply, it occurred to me that my supervisor had reminded me strongly of a favourite aunt whom I had been very close to as a child. I had found myself unconsciously responding to my supervisor as I had done to my aunt (transference). This triggered an unconscious response in my supervisor (counter-transference). She became aware of this counter-transference through her own strong (and uncharacteristic) response to me. By making the transference and counter-transference transparent, we were able to move on and create a meaningful relationship of our own. Shohet (2011) suggests that transference can often play a part in professional helping relationships, counselling and supervision. A patient/healer transference and counter-transference may develop where the 'patient' unconsciously looks to the 'healer' to make them well (transference), and the 'healer' finds themselves feeling responsible for restoring their 'patient' to full health (counter-transference). It is therefore often helpful to ask the question *Who am I to you?* or *Who are you, to me?* when powerful feelings emerge.

REFLECTION POINT

Try to remember a time when you had a strong response to someone on a first meeting. It might be an authority figure, a colleague, a client or someone you have met socially. What provoked this response? After all, you did not know this person. And how did they respond to you? Ask yourself the question *Who is this person to me?* or *What does this person represent?* It could be, if they are an authority figure, that you are transferring feelings engendered by authority figures in your childhood – parents, teachers and so on. Likewise, meeting new colleagues, clients or acquaintances could trigger unconscious memories of relationships in the past. If so, this may influence your response to these individuals in the here and now. The presence of a strong emotional response on initial meeting suggests that transference and counter-transference is present.

So, to return to Theo's work with her three supervisees, each at a different level in Stoltenberg et al.'s model, let us think about how we might progress their development, possibly by using transference positively. Whiting et al. (2001) suggest strategies for encouraging supervisees to progress through the developmental stages, and we will consider these in a moment, but first, take time to reflect on what you might do in each case.

ACTIVITY 7.1

Go back to Case study 7.1. If you were Theo, what would you do in supervision to enable Sian, Jonah and Vrinda to continue to develop as supervisees? Make some notes and then compare them with what follows.

The role of the supervisor at each stage is outlined below. So in each case Theo might do the following.

- *Level one* Take time to focus on the nature of the supervisory relationship. It can be helpful to explore the normative, formative and restorative functions, so that Sian develops a clearer idea of what supervision sets out to achieve, thus reducing the anxiety she is experiencing. It may also be appropriate for Theo to ask Sian: *Who am I to you?* to begin to explore any emerging issues of transference and counter-transference. This might be helpful in encouraging Sian to think about transference in her counselling practice in the future. Sian will benefit from positive feedback on her practice in order to help her feel more confident about the skills she is developing. Challenge at this stage should be tentative and not confrontational. As well as recognising the strengths in Sian's practice (restorative function), it is also important to attend to the formative function whereby attention is paid to developing new skills and strategies, using words such as: *You say that you sometimes feel you are going round in circles with your client. I wonder if it might be a good idea to use the skill of summary a little more. How might that help to maintain a focus?*

- *Level two* Encourage Jonah to begin to conceptualise the work with clients rather than simply describe what he is doing. For example, Theo might ask Jonah: *Tell me what is going on in the room when you are with your client* in order to examine possible issues of transference/counter-transference in the counselling relationship. The task here is to encourage a more objective analysis of the work and to enable a deeper understanding. Use of the parallel process can be helpful at this stage. Theo might say: *As you describe your work with this client, I'm finding it very difficult to grasp exactly what is happening in your sessions. Everything feels a little cloudy. I wonder if this is how your client is feeling too? A little muddled, a bit confused?*

- *Level three* Continue to work collaboratively with Vrinda, encouraging and supporting her reflections on her practice. As with Jonah, ask Vrinda to use conceptual frameworks to articulate the work, drawing more widely on the theoretical orientation underpinning her counselling practice. At this level, supervisees might be encouraged to work more creatively with their clients, developing advanced techniques and strategies. Theo might consider using creative approaches in supervision (see Chapter 8) for two reasons: to encourage Vrinda to gain new perspectives on her client practice and to enable her to develop more creative approaches in her own counselling work with clients.

The developmental approach described above, the characteristics of each level and the suggestions offered for encouraging supervisees to progress are all helpful. 'Stuckness' and even resistance can be a feature of supervision, just as it is in counselling. Taking a moment to reflect on how effectively the supervisee is developing through the process can provide a helpful starting point for examining feelings of inertia or antipathy in supervision and suggest a way forward. Of course, as is the case with any theoretical concept, the efficacy of Stoltenberg et al.'s developmental approach has been challenged. Ellis and Ladany (1997) point out that there is no evidence to support the underpinning assumptions about supervisees' development. They suggest there is a need for further testing in order to gain empirical evidence about supervisees' transformations through the process of supervision. This is an important point, but it should not imply that reflecting on supervisees' development is of little value. Whiting et al. explain that developmental perspectives *assist the profession in continuing our conceptualisations and conclusions about the process of becoming a mature clinician* (2001, p144).

So far, we have examined the development of supervisees through supervision, paying attention to the different levels through which they progress. The supervisee's development may also provide a clue to evaluating how effectively the supervisory relationship is progressing. It is the supervisor's (and supervisee's) responsibility to reflect on any blocks or barriers that are hindering the development of the relationship between them. These may be, in part, due to the level that the supervisee is at in their own development or they may be to do with the *process* of supervision. So another concept worthy of deeper examination, which also offers a guide to understanding and progressing the supervisory relationship, is the process of supervision itself. Hawkins and Shohet (2006) describe a seven-eyed model that sets out to encapsulate this process clearly.

The seven-eyed process model

Hawkins and Shohet's 'double-matrix' or seven-eyed supervisor model was introduced in Chapter 3. Unlike Stoltenberg et al.'s focus on the supervisee, this model seeks to identify the key features of the supervision process, thereby illuminating the relationship between supervisor and supervisee further. To recap, the model suggests key 'modes' that should be present in supervision. These modes form the 'seven eyes' of the model. They are:

- *the client* – although not 'present' in the room, client work is at the heart of supervision practice;

- *strategies and interventions* – the type of interventions used by the supervisee in counselling, examining strategies and skills used and working to develop new intervention approaches;

- *the relationship between client and supervisee* – an examination of the conscious and unconscious responses and dynamic within the relationship between the supervisee and their client in order to develop as more reflexive counsellors;

- *the supervisee* – the ways in which the supervisee is affected by the work with clients; developing greater self-awareness by, for example, exploring issues of transference and counter-transference;

- *the supervisory relationship* – how the relationship between supervisor and supervisee is progressing, identifying any barriers and attending to these in supervision and, in particular, considering issues of parallel process in supervision and client work;

- *the supervisor* – paying attention to the feelings, thoughts and images experienced by the supervisor in supervision sessions, including a heightened awareness of issues of transference and counter-transference in the supervision relationship;

- *the wider context* – attending to the range of contexts that are 'present' in both supervision and client work, including understanding the 'wider world' of supervisor, supervisee and client, and taking into account the concept of cultural 'difference'.

Hawkins and Shohet do not intend the model to be used as a checklist for supervision whereby the supervisor asks in turn about the client, the interventions, the relationship, the supervisee, the supervisory relationship, and so on. Rather, the model suggests components that should be integrated within the supervision process. Activity 7.2 illustrates three supervision sessions where the supervisor is demonstrating an awareness of the seven eyes identified above.

ACTIVITY 7.2

In each of the following scenarios, can you spot which mode or 'eye' is being attended to?

Supervisor A: *I notice that we've spent a lot of time this session talking about the issue you are having with some of your colleagues in the team . . . in particular the frustrations you are experiencing when we meet for group supervision. It's important that you have the opportunity to air your concerns, although we should be mindful that supervision is primarily about client work. Which of your clients would you like to bring to today's session?*

Supervisor B: *You have painted a really clear picture of your client today. I'm getting a real sense of who they are and the issues they are bringing to counselling. It might be helpful to move on now and examine more fully the work in your counselling sessions with this client. What actually happens and how do you find yourself feeling about and responding to this client?*

Supervisor C: *I'm aware that I'm feeling that something's not quite right here today. I don't know . . . I might be wrong . . . but we seem to be fighting against each other rather than working together. What do you think? Are you feeling that too?*

Each intervention outlined above demonstrates how the supervisor's awareness of the seven-eyed model is helping to progress the supervision work. Supervisor A is reminding the supervisee that the client should be 'present' in supervision. Supervisor B is concerned with encouraging the supervisee to explore and develop the interventions that are taking place in counselling and the supervisee's relationship with the client, while supervisor C is using the skill of immediacy to examine the 'block' that seems to have developed in the supervisory relationship.

REFLECTION POINT

Take a moment to think about your own experience of supervision. As you reflect on the modes identified above, identify any 'eyes' that you feel have remained shut or that are, perhaps, half-open. Here are examples.

- How much are clients present in your supervision sessions?
- To what extent are interventions between supervisee and client explored?
- How much is the relationship between the two examined?
- How highly developed is the supervisee's self-awareness?
- How much does the supervisor know and understand the supervisee?
- To what extent is the relationship between supervisor and supervisee discussed?
- How far does the supervisor reflect on their own responses to what is being brought to supervision?
- How much is the wider context of the work present 'in the room' in supervision sessions?

If you are a practising supervisor and you are aware of a mode or modes here that are not being attended to in supervision sessions, then you have the opportunity now to think about how you might effect change. If you are reflecting as a supervisee and can identify areas that you feel have been neglected in your own supervision, you might want to consider how you could raise these with your supervisor in the future.

To summarise this section, when reflecting on how effectively the relationship between supervisor and supervisee is progressing, it is helpful to consider developmental models that inform our understanding. This book introduces three such developmental models, and this chapter explores their application further.

- The five-stage model that focuses on the development of the *relationship* between supervisor and supervisee.

- Stoltenberg et al.'s IDM developmental model that charts the features of the development of the *supervisee* through the supervision process.

- Hawkins and Shohet's seven-eyed process model that offers us a means to understand the *process* of supervision.

Having examined how key theories and concepts underpinning the development of the supervisory relationship are applied, it is helpful to reflect too on how communication between supervisor and supervisee can be optimised in order to ensure that the relationship progresses effectively. After all, effective communication is what supervision (like counselling) is all about. But any examination of communication should be informed by an awareness of potential power dynamics that may be present in the relationship. Shohet and Wilmot (1991) suggest that, like it or not, the relationship between supervisor and supervisee may be perceived as that of expert and novice. Feltham (2002b) goes further, highlighting the perception of supervision as a surveillance activity. To address these fears – and ensure that a relationship adhering to the core conditions of empathy, congruence and unconditional positive regard is built (see Chapter 6) – the method of communication between supervisor and supervisee is worthy of examination. Berne's (1964) theory of transactional analysis offers a helpful insight into effective communication and will be explored further here.

TRANSACTIONAL ANALYSIS

The concept of transactional analysis may already be familiar as it is often introduced as part of counsellor training. Tudor and Sills (2012) offer a helpful overview, and Westergaard (2011) examines how knowledge of TA is helpful in counselling with young people. Put simply, TA offers a theory of communication, based in the psychoanalytic tradition, whereby the significance of the unconscious is recognised in the ways in which we 'transact' with each other. It also acknowledges the principles of the person-centred approach, respecting that individuals are capable of change. There are a number of key concepts explored in TA, including the significance of ego states, the existence of life scripts and the playing of games or 'rackets'. Here we will examine the features of the approach that focus primarily on communication: the ego states.

The ego states

Berne suggested that we communicate on two levels: the social level and the psychological level. The social level is the conscious selecting of the words we use, and the psychological level is the often unconscious messages we are delivering through our tone of voice, facial expressions, body posture and other non-verbal cues. Berne emphasised the importance of unconscious communication and advocated attending to the whole person in counselling, using all our senses: sight, sound, touch, taste and feel. Berne went on to suggest that we have access to three ego states from which we can communicate. These are:

- parent;
- adult;
- child.

Communication from different ego states is generally an unconscious process. Westergaard describes the ego states thus:

> *Parent ego state*
> *The Parent ego state is learned, from birth, and is a manifestation of our observations of our own parent's or parental figure's behaviour and responses. This ego state is subdivided into two: the Critical Parent (CP) and the Nurturing Parent (NP). Communication from the Critical Parent ego state is likely to be characterised by a sharp tone of voice, a pointing finger, a stern expression. For example: 'Don't you ever do that again!' or 'You're late again! You must make sure you're here on time in future.' The Nurturing Parent is very different in tone to the Critical Parent, but is learned in exactly the same way through observation of parents and parental figures as a child. A response coming from a Nurturing Parent ego state might sound like this: 'Oh you poor thing, come here and I'll sort it out for you.' Or: 'Tell me all about it and I'll make sure that never happens again.' The Nurturing Parent ego state is often characterised by gentleness of tone, softness of facial expression and openness of body posture. Communication from the Nurturing Parent suggests a 'there there, let me make it better' response which can appear comforting, but is not necessarily helpful in enabling the recipient to manage their life more effectively for themselves.*
>
> *Child ego state*
> *As with the Parent, transactions from the Child ego state present from two different perspectives: the Free Child (FC) and the Adapted Child (AC). Communication from our Free Child (FC) is spontaneous, curious, creative or rebellious. A typically Free Child response might sound like this: 'OK, the sun's shining. Let's forget about going to work today and go to the beach instead!' Or: 'There's no way anyone is going to tell me what to do, it's my*

life, it's up to me!' By contrast, in the Adapted Child (AC) ego state, communications stem from a willingness to please, to agree and to 'do the right thing'. Someone responding to the two Free Child examples above from their Adapted Child might say to the first 'I'd love to go to the beach, but I don't want to get into trouble and get told off,' and to the second 'I wish I could do what I want like you, but I'm afraid that life's just not like that for me.'

Adult ego state
The third ego state is that of Adult. Transactions from the Adult ego state suggest a logical, rational and assertive response, firmly rooted in the 'here and now.' When communication stems from our Adult it will be reasoned, clear and underpinned by a sense of self-responsibility. We have access to all three ego states from around the age of 10 to 12 years.

(Westergaard, 2011, pp81–83)

So in a supervisory relationship, it is important to listen actively to both the social and the psychological communication that is taking place. Generally, in helping relationships the focus is on objective and analytical communication in order to explore issues and find strategies and ways forward. That should not suggest that communication is without emotion – far from it – but rather that emotional responses are recognised and explored. This suggests that in supervision, it is helpful to communicate from the Adult ego state. The example below shows a 'transaction' between supervisor and supervisee from three different perspectives.

ACTIVITY 7.3

Read the response of each supervisor to the supervisee who is communicating from the Child ego state. Which ego state is the supervisor communicating from in each case? Which response do you think is likely to be most effective?

Supervisee: *I just don't know what to do. It's happened again. I knew it would. I'm just not getting anywhere with this client. It's hopeless!*

Response 1: Supervisor: *Yes, we do keep coming back to this client time after time, don't we? Why don't you just try something different with her?*

Response 2: Supervisor: *I know just what you mean. I had a client just like that myself. Nightmare!*

Response 3: Supervisor: *I can see how tough this is for you. As you say, you are feeling hopeless right now. Let's think a little more about this stuckness and see if we can identify a way forward.*

Clearly, response three is likely to be the most effective. That is because it comes from the Adult ego state and therefore it will encourage the supervisee to move from their Child to their Adult in response and begin to engage with a more analytical conversation concerned with understanding what is happening and finding a way forward.

REFLECTION POINT

Take a moment to reflect on your current relationship with your supervisor/supervisee (if you are in counselling training and have not yet received supervision, you might want to think about your relationship with your tutor instead). Can you identify which ego state dominates the communication between you in your sessions?

It is likely that you identified the Adult ego state as being predominant in supervision. This means that you are working collaboratively and effectively together. If the Child or Parent ego states are present frequently in sessions, then it is likely that either supervisor or supervisee is not communicating assertively, but is taking an aggressive or passive approach to the work. This may indicate underlying issues of transference and counter-transference. Where this is the case, exploration of what is happening within the relationship is helpful, and attendance to breaking the pattern that has emerged by staying in Adult is likely to help the situation move forward.

So knowledge of the ego states offers us a means to analyse communication in supervision (and in client work in counselling) and progress towards assertive Adult to Adult transactions. TA is not a technique or a model that supervisors and counsellors 'do' in practice. Rather, it is a way of standing back, reflecting on, understanding and analysing what is happening in the relationship at both a social and psychological level.

STAGE THREE: PROGRESSING THE SUPERVISORY RELATIONSHIP

ACTIVITY 7.4

Let us return to our three supervisory relationships (introduced in Chapters 5 and 6) and discover how effectively the supervisory relationship is developing in each case. As you read the case studies that follow, reflect on the key concepts examined in this chapter. Try to establish the level of each supervisee's development, the effectiveness of the process and any barriers that appear to have emerged. Finally, examine the quality of communication in each case.

Case study 7.2 Mark and Bridget

Mark and Bridget have met on six occasions. Although this is Mark's first experience of supervision as a supervisor, he is feeling increasingly confident and comfortable in the role. He is aware that his initial fears of not being 'good enough' for Bridget, who is an experienced counsellor, were largely unfounded, although he sometimes finds himself reluctant to challenge Bridget for fear of 'getting it wrong'. Things seemed to settle down after the second session where Mark and Bridget agreed a supervision contract (this had been overlooked in the first session). Bridget is enjoying her supervision with Mark. She feels supported, although sometimes she suspects that Mark tends to agree with her when she would like an alternative perspective on her work. She is, however, finding that Mark's person-centred approach is helping her to develop more reflexively by staying in the 'here and now' in terms of her own feelings and responses to her clients. Bridget uses the time productively and comes away feeling that she has been given an opportunity to reflect on her client work. She is not sure that she is gaining new perspectives as she is not conceptualising her practice in relation to other theoretical frameworks that she uses as an integrative counsellor. She feels a little frustrated that she is not learning and developing new strategies to use in her work, but she is aware that she has not vocalised these feelings because Mark is so new to supervision and she does not want to challenge him so early on in their relationship.

Case study 7.3 Fran and Gemma

Gemma, a counsellor in training, has also had six sessions with her supervisor Fran. When Gemma first met Fran, she was just about to begin working with clients at her placement at the local college. Initially Fran had encouraged Gemma to share her feelings concerning meeting clients for the first time. Gemma found it helpful to discuss her fears and anxieties with Fran who was very easy to talk to. However, Fran is conscious that now Gemma has started to work with clients she needs plenty of reassurance. Gemma often says things like *I did that wrong, didn't I?* or *I think I might have messed up* or *You don't think that's right, do you?* Supervision tends to focus on Gemma telling the clients' 'stories' rather than engaging at a deeper level with the underpinning issues. Fran knows that this is to be expected with supervisees who are new to counselling (and supervision). However, after the last session together, Fran is aware that at one point during the session she had experienced an urge to snap *I'm not an expert, you know! I don't have all the answers.* On reflection, she feels that it might be helpful to take time in their next session together to review the purpose of supervision and share how they are both feeling the relationship is developing.

Case study 7.4 Karen and Clive

Karen and Clive's relationship got off to a rocky start. Clive could not see the point of negotiating a contract with his new supervisor, and Karen left the session without asking for payment. These issues were resolved in session two when Karen suggested they think long and hard about whether they should continue to work together. They have now had five sessions, and the relationship has developed very effectively. Clive finds Karen's psychodynamic approach to counselling interesting and enlightening in their discussions about client work. Although he is a CBT-trained counsellor, he has been surprised to discover how much he has learned about his counselling practice with a psychodynamically trained supervisor. Karen too has been pleased to see how positively Clive has used the time together. He is insightful and open about his work with clients. There is one thing, though, that Karen has become aware of in supervision: Clive does not demonstrate reflexiveness in relation to his practice. He seems to find it hard to examine the part he plays in his client work. This is something that Karen is trying to address, but she is aware that the supervisory relationship must develop further to a point where Clive can trust her enough to really open up about himself within the work.

It is clear that each supervisory relationship is developing. Mark and Bridget are beginning to engage with discussions about client work, although Mark's inexperience as a supervisor means that challenge is an issue. Interestingly, Bridget too is finding it difficult to challenge Mark. There may be issues of transference/counter-transference developing here. It appears that Bridget has already reached level three of Stoltenberg et al.'s model. She has excellent reflexive skills and seems to have a well-developed 'internal supervisor'. In relation to Hawkins and Shohet's seven-eyed model, it is the relationship between supervisor and supervisee that is, perhaps, worthy of discussion, in order to enable both parties to move on from stage three, 'progressing' to stage four, the 'working alliance' phase of the supervisory relationship.

In the case of Fran and Gemma, the development of the supervisee is at level one in Stoltenberg et al.'s model. This is not surprising. Not only is this Gemma's first experience of supervision, but she is also counselling clients for the first time too. In order to help Gemma and the supervisory relationship to progress, Fran plans to go back and explore the purpose and functions of supervision in more depth. She might also consider introducing the concept of the parallel process, encouraging Gemma to reflect on how clients might feel and what they may expect when they see a counsellor for the first time. Fran is also aware of her desire to respond to Gemma from her Critical Parent ego state. This may suggest that Gemma is communicating from her Child. Fran reflects on this and reminds herself of the importance of staying in her Adult in order to develop assertive communication between them in subsequent sessions. In addition, she plans to share her insight and knowledge of TA to enable Gemma to explore feelings about supervision and her counselling work.

Karen and Clive, after a shaky start, have engaged well with the supervision process. In spite of their different theoretical orientations, positive work is taking place. On reflection, Karen feels that one 'eye' in Hawkins and Shohet's seven-eyed model seems reluctant to open: Clive's level of reflexivity. Karen wonders if this is something to do with the differences in orientation, her own being psychodynamic and Clive's being cognitive behavioural. But she is aware too that regardless of orientation, counsellors should develop reflexive skills, refining the ability to consider themselves in relation to their work with clients. The supervisory relationship must continue to progress in order to reach the next phase of its development: the working alliance.

In the next chapter we will examine stage four of the supervisory relationship model: the working alliance. We will return to Mark and Bridget, Fran and Gemma, and Karen and Clive to discover if and how they have managed to achieve a working alliance in their relationships.

CHAPTER SUMMARY

This chapter focused on the elements underpinning the successful progression of a supervisory relationship. It examined:

- developmental theories, including Stoltenberg et al.'s three levels of supervisee development (IDM)and Hawkins and Shohet's seven-eyed process model;

- the concept of transference and counter-transference as a means for understanding supervisory (and counselling) relationships more effectively;

- a way of analysing communication by using TA, considering both social and psychological communication and identifying the significance of ego states.

To progress the relationship effectively to the working alliance stage (see Chapter 8), both supervisor and supervisee will recognise, negotiate and work hard to overcome any barriers and resistance between them. They will have understood the purpose of supervision and found a 'way of being' together that acknowledges the developmental nature of the process.

SUGGESTED FURTHER READING

Bradley, L J and Ladany, N (2001) *Counselor supervision: principles, process and practice*. Philadelphia PA: Brunner-Routledge.

Chapter 2 of this text examines the development of the supervisory relationship, in particular the development of the supervisee through the process.

Feltham, C and Horton, I (eds) (2012) *The Sage handbook of counselling and psychotherapy*, 3rd edition. London: Sage.

Part 5.1 of this comprehensive counselling handbook focuses on psychoanalytic therapy and examines the concepts of transference and counter-transference, while part 5.23 provides an overview of transactional analysis.

Hawkins, P and Shohet, R (2006) *Supervision in the helping professions*, 3rd edition. Milton Keynes: Open University Press.

This text has been recommended in other chapters in this book, but it is particularly relevant here as the seven-eyed process model is explored in depth in Chapter 7.

CHAPTER 8

Maintaining a working alliance in supervision

Jane Westergaard

CORE KNOWLEDGE

This chapter will provide the opportunity to:

- examine the features of the working alliance phase;
- clarify the supervisory tasks of feeding back and prescribing;
- identify the skills of challenge and immediacy;
- explore the use of creative methods in one-to-one and group supervision.

INTRODUCTION

Chapters 5 to 7 of this book introduce a supervisory relationship model that examines how to prepare for supervision and, subsequently, establish and progress the relationship between supervisor and supervisee. This chapter moves on to focus on the next stage of development of the supervisory relationship: the working alliance phase. Reynolds (2006) highlights the parallel between the working alliance in counselling and supervision, emphasising the need for joint working and the creation of an empathic learning environment in both activities.

This chapter examines what constitutes a working alliance, identifying the features and characteristics of this stage of the relationship. It goes on to highlight two tasks that are central to supervision but are less apparent in counselling relationships with clients: prescribing and feeding back. It also identifies the skills of challenge and immediacy, which supervisors use to develop deeper reflexivity in the working alliance stage. The chapter continues by examining the use of creative methods in supervision (both in individual and group supervision) in order to encourage supervisees to conceptualise and develop their understanding and practice further. Finally, we return to our three supervisory relationships to reflect on how effectively the working alliance stage has been negotiated by Mark and Bridget, Fran and Gemma, and Karen and Clive.

KEY FEATURES OF THE WORKING ALLIANCE STAGE OF THE SUPERVISORY RELATIONSHIP

Holloway (1995) describes a 'mature' phase of the supervisory relationship and identifies a range of characteristics that might suggest that a higher level of trust and intimacy has developed between supervisor and supervisee. Before sharing Holloway's thoughts on what constitutes a working alliance, take a moment to identify what you think should be present at the mature or working alliance stage of supervision.

ACTIVITY 8.1

Make a list of key words that, for you, exemplify a working alliance stage of a helping relationship. Remember that the term 'working alliance' is present in both counselling and supervision, and that the words you select may be informed by both your counselling and supervision experience. If you have not yet received supervision, reflect on other 'helping' relationships you have experienced currently or in the past – perhaps through your own therapy, or as a trainee counsellor with fellow students or tutors.

It is likely that your list includes words such as 'trust', 'honesty' and 'respect', expressions that summarise the 'safe space' present in an effective supervisory relationship. There may also be more dynamic terms such as 'risk-taking', 'challenge' and 'creative'. This terminology suggests that the relationship has moved on to a deeper level whereby there is less imperative to disguise feelings of vulnerability in supervision and more willingness to share doubts, admit mistakes and be open to trying out new approaches. Holloway summarises the mature phase of the relationship as 'individualised'. She suggests that both supervisor and supervisee are less constrained by their 'roles' in the relationship (perhaps as 'teacher' and 'student' or 'expert' and 'novice') and are operating more as two professionals who are working in collaboration and learning with each other. Dependency on the supervisor to offer an 'expert' view has shifted to greater autonomy and the development of the internal supervisor within the supervisee. In the case study below, Robert and Jacob describe their experiences of the working alliance stage of their supervisory relationship.

Case study 8.1 Robert and Jacob

Robert (supervisor): *I've been working with Jacob for over two years. During that time I'd say our relationship has developed enormously. When I think back to our early sessions, I almost can't recognise the Jacob then compared with the Jacob now. Initially he was nervous, anxious, very tentative about offering his thoughts and feelings concerning his client work. Now, he is open, curious, able to challenge himself – and me! He has developed his skills of reflection and works both intuitively and reflexively – with real insight. He is willing to take risks in supervision too. Recently we have tried out some creative approaches to help to conceptualise his work and develop a deeper understanding. This has been enlightening – for us both.*

Jacob (supervisee): *Robert is great! At first I was in awe of him, to be honest. I'm not saying that this isn't the case any more, but I'd describe our relationship now as mutually respectful rather than awe-inspiring. I love how Robert challenges me to think in different ways, and to try out new approaches in my work with clients. There are times when I think 'No, that won't work', but I can articulate my feelings and we've had some intense and enlightening discussions. We've literally 'tried things out' in supervision using role play, Gestalt techniques and other creative methods. I'm always really excited by the insight I've gained when we do this. Mind you, if Robert had suggested these techniques earlier in the relationship I would probably have run for the hills.*

What is striking here is the energy evident in both testimonies. There is a clear sense that the relationship has moved from one of teacher–student to a collaborative and fully engaged partnership. This resonates with Holloway's vision of a strong emotional bond between supervisor and supervisee, and exemplifies the true meaning of the word 'alliance'. In brief, the following components indicate that the working alliance stage of supervision has been reached.

- *High levels of trust*: this suggests honest and open two-way communication. Initial anxiety has been overcome, the boundaries are clearly established and the relationship has been tested. Both supervisor and supervisee trust themselves and each other in the supervisory relationship.

- *Greater autonomy on behalf of the supervisee*: the supervisee is developing their 'internal supervisor' whereby supervision is an ongoing reflexive process that continues outside the formal sessions with the supervisor. Supervisees come to supervision with a clear agenda and engage actively and thoughtfully in the work, with little prompting from the supervisor.

- *A willingness to be vulnerable and admit mistakes*: both supervisee and supervisor demonstrate their reflexive approach to the work, reflecting on their own position in relation to the other, to clients and to the work. This means being open enough to reveal uncertainty and vulnerability. It also demonstrates the ability to reflect on and question decisions made and approaches used in both supervision and counselling practice.

- *A positive response to being challenged*: both parties are able to accept challenge as a helpful and constructive element of supervision. Challenge should not suggest or be viewed as confrontation or accusation, but rather as an opportunity for deeper reflection, curiosity and critical analysis of practice and self.

- *Self-disclosure*: it is important that levels of trust between supervisee and supervisor can sustain disclosure of personal and emotional responses influencing either the supervisory relationship or counselling work with clients. Self-disclosure should always be undertaken with person-centred principles in mind; the question 'How will this help?' should be aired before disclosures are made.

- *A willingness to take risks in the work*: in order to move any relationship on to a deeper level, there will be elements of risk-taking present. This should not imply undertaking 'risky' activities either in counselling or supervision. But rather risk-taking suggests an openness to engaging with alternative approaches and using immediacy in the work while making greater use of 'self' in both the supervisory and counselling relationship.

- *A willingness to engage with creative approaches*: creativity is associated strongly with the notion of play; curiosity and playfulness are concepts that have underpinned therapeutic work for some time (Winnicott, 1971), and can be used effectively in supervision as well as in counselling practice.

REFLECTION POINT

Take a moment to reflect on your own supervision (either as a supervisor or supervisee). To what extent would you say that the elements outlined above are present in your current supervision (or have been in past supervisory relationships)? Were any missing? What might you or your supervisor do to move the relationship forward to the working alliance stage? If you have not received supervision yet, the list may appear daunting. It might help to reflect again on current helping relationships with which you are engaged. To what extent are the elements listed here present in other helping relationships?

Achieving the working alliance stage of the supervisory relationship is neither simple nor straightforward. It is not something that happens naturally as a consequence of engaging in X number of supervision sessions over a period of time. However, if the conditions are right, the working alliance can develop quickly.

Initially, it may seem to the new supervisor that issues such as self-disclosure, risk-taking and creativity are too challenging to contemplate. This is not surprising. In the same way that counsellors are unlikely to introduce creative methods in their early counselling sessions, it takes time to develop the confidence in the relationship and the work to progress to the working alliance stage. Rapisarda et al. (2011), undertaking research with trainee supervisors, discovered that their students used their own experiences of supervision as supervisees as a guide to 'model' their work as supervisors. This is helpful, as it reminds us that in order to become a supervisor we must first have received supervision, and we will have learned much from our experiences as a supervisee. Rapisarda et al.'s research with trainee supervisors also identified key supervision tasks that appeared to stimulate a climate in which supervisees could grow and develop their practice. If carried out effectively, these tasks should also contribute to the building of a supervisory working alliance. The tasks are:

- building structure in sessions;
- enabling supervisee development;
- sharing critical feedback.

The first two tasks were identified by the trainee supervisors as less problematic. The parallel between counselling work with clients and supervision with supervisees is evident here. The third task, giving feedback, was considered more challenging to manage. One participant described how they gave feedback to their supervisee by saying *No, this is not wrong, this was good, but there's more you can do* (Rapisarda et al., 2011, p116). This is a helpful response that should serve to engage rather than alienate the supervisee while keeping supervision positive. However, 'finding the right words' can be problematic, and in order to reach the working alliance stage of the supervisory relationship, the task of feeding back and, at times, prescribing practice must be successfully negotiated – but how?

Prescribing best practice and offering feedback: using challenge and immediacy

Although much emphasis has been placed throughout this book on the concept of the parallel processes in counselling and supervision, it is important to remember that there are key differences between each activity. These differences are, in the main, related to the *normative* function of supervision (Inskipp and Proctor, 1993) whereby the supervisee's practice must adhere to legal, ethical and policy-related guidelines and requirements. To this extent it could be argued that the supervisory relationship is more directive than the counselling relationship. Indeed, counsellors rarely tell their clients *What you are doing is wrong and must stop*. Those words are unlikely to be uttered in quite that way in supervision, either, but it is important to understand that there is a requirement for supervisors to ensure that their supervisees are working safely, ethically and within the law. Let us think about times when we may need to feed back constructive criticism or even prescribe our supervisee's practice.

ACTIVITY 8.2

Read the scenarios set out below and reflect on what you have already read in Chapter 2 concerning ethical practice. Make notes about how you would respond in each case. Write down the actual words you would use rather than a general 'Yes, I would challenge' response.

1. Your supervisee discloses that she has arranged to meet socially a client with whom she has recently ended a counselling relationship.

2. Your supervisee tells you that on a number of occasions he has given money to a young client who is destitute.

3. Your supervisee discloses that he has known for some time that there is an issue of ongoing domestic violence with a couple he is counselling who have young children.

4. Your supervisee has given his phone number to a client who is suicidal. This goes against the policy of the organisation that employs him as a counsellor.

We will return to these scenarios later, once we have explored the tasks of prescribing and feeding back and examined the skills of challenge and immediacy, to see if our responses to these situations have changed.

The task of prescribing practice is, as already stated, tricky for many, because of its connotations of 'getting it wrong' and being 'told off'. This can provoke feelings that most of us find challenging to process because of previous painful or unresolved experiences of being corrected, chastised or told what to do. Our understanding of transactional analysis and transference and counter-transference, explored in Chapter 7, should help us to locate feelings engendered by constructive criticism or direction. But that does not necessarily make it any easier to accept that in some way we must develop or change our practice. In order to reflect on the ways in which supervisees' work can be directed effectively, Heron (1975) developed a six-category intervention analysis. This provides a helpful framework for analysing *enabling interventions* (of which supervision is one). The first three categories he termed *authoritative* the second three, *facilitative*. He explained that helping relationships involve the following types of intervention.

Authoritative interventions

• *Prescriptive*: be direct in your advice, for example: *You must stop seeing your client outside the counselling relationship* or *You must complete your counselling notes after every session.*

• *Informative*: instruct, explain or provide information, for example: *Locate the agency policy that sets out the regulations regarding contact with clients outside of counselling* or *Ask the office manager to clarify the format of your counselling notes and where to file them.*

• *Confrontative*: challenge, for example: *How will you manage this breach in boundary with your client?* or *We've talked about your counselling notes before. What is the difficulty you seem to be experiencing?*

Facilitative interventions

• *Cathartic*: helping to release tension and emotion, for example: *I get the feeling that work with this client has raised particular emotional issues for you.* or *When we talk about your client notes, it seems to me that you become very defensive. Is that how it is?*

• *Catalytic*: encouraging problem-solving and ownership, for example: *Can you tell me a bit more about how working with this client has made you feel?* or *What could you do to ensure that you write up your counselling notes after every session?*

• *Supportive*: affirming the self-worth of the supervisee, for example: *I can see how difficult the situation with this client has been for you* or *Your insight about your client work in supervision is impressive. Recording this in your client notes will be so helpful for the agency.*

Heron's six categories of intervention within the broad sub-headings of authoritative and facilitative offer a helpful way to analyse interactions in counselling as well as supervision. It is likely that counsellors identify that their work resides largely under the facilitative sub-heading, and it is for this reason that the authoritative interventions may feel unfamiliar at best and uncomfortable at worst to new supervisors. But Heron is careful to stress that each category of intervention applies to helping relationships, and therefore factors such as tone, body language, demeanour and approach play an important part. For example, a prescriptive intervention that is accompanied by a bark and a frown is not an enabling response at all and, therefore, not appropriate within the context of a helping relationship.

ACTIVITY 8.3

Reflect on a recent supervision session (it can be helpful to audio-record sessions, but you must seek advice on this first from your counselling agency). Analyse the interaction using Heron's six-category intervention framework. You might begin by reflecting on the broader sub-headings. Would you identify your approach as mostly authoritative or facilitative? Which of the interventions, if any, dominate your work? Were there times that, on reflection, you should have taken a more prescriptive, informative or confrontative approach? If you have not yet started supervising, you might want to reflect on which type of intervention you think you might find most challenging when you begin to supervise.

It might be helpful to discuss your analysis with your own supervisor and reflect on any barriers you are facing in developing direct communication and constructive criticism with your supervisee. In addition to prescribing or directing, feeding back on elements of practice is central to supervision. The supervisor who struggles with offering critical feedback is unlikely to be fulfilling the functions of supervision. Breene summarises her thoughts about the challenges of giving feedback in supervision:

> *From the panic I see in faces when feedback is mentioned, I imagine it is equated with negative criticism, often deriving from experiences of receiving feedback that were shaming, humiliating. Of course people will resist that and close down . . .*

She goes on:

> *So I suggest asking the person who is to receive the feedback three short questions: 'What do you think worked?' Where did you get stuck?' and 'What might you do differently next time?' This empties their cup before you pour in your huge jug of marvellous comments – or helps you realise that they know all or most of what you were going to say anyway.*
>
> (Breene, 2011, p177)

Hawkins and Shohet (2006) agree that offering feedback can be a difficult aspect of supervision. They suggest the pneumonic CORBS as a guide to providing feeding back positively.

- Clear: be direct and not ambiguous.

- Owned: remember your feedback is based on your perceptions. Be assertive and 'own' your words. This avoids a feeling of blame.

- *Regular*: do not 'collect stamps' and cash them in all at once. In other words, ensure that feedback is given regularly rather than put off until the issue has escalated.

- *Balanced*: ensure that a balance is maintained between positive and negative feedback.

- *Specific*: avoid making generalised comments. Feedback should be 'backed up' with specific examples where possible.

Hawkins and Shohet also make the point that receiving feedback is not a passive process, and supervisees should be encouraged to offer their own feedback with regard to their practice and to the process of supervision.

So prescribing practice and feeding back are activities central to supervision. And there are two skills in particular that help us to direct, question and provide feedback to supervisees while maintaining a positive relationship. These skills are challenge and immediacy. Both skills will be familiar to counsellors, but here they are discussed in the context of supervision practice.

Challenge

As already stated, the skill of challenge should not imply a criticism, a confrontation or a 'ticking off'. Instead, challenge encourages supervisees to stop, reflect, question, analyse and make adjustments or develop their practice appropriately. Challenge is made up of a number of different skills identified below.

- *Helpful questions*: asking open questions such as *What was the thinking behind your decision? How did you reach that conclusion?* and *What were the consequences of your actions?* can be helpful in encouraging self-challenge. The supervisor is asking the supervisee to reach their own conclusions and offer their own rationale for the element of their practice requiring a challenge. A constructive dialogue can then ensue.

- *Reflection*: sometimes reflecting back and emphasising one key word can serve as a challenge, for example: *You say that sometimes you hate working with this client?* 'Hate' is a powerful word, and to hear it back will challenge the supervisee to clarify and express their feelings more fully.

- *Summarising*: it can be helpful to summarise what has been said, particularly if the supervisor senses a discrepancy inherent in the supervisee's discussion of practice, for example: *You told me earlier that your client presents as very angry and withdrawn in counselling. You say that it is difficult to 'find a way in'. Just now, though, you said that your client became very animated and excited when you asked about her current situation at work. What might that tell you?* By using the supervisee's own words and 'offering them back' the supervisor is challenging the supervisee, providing time and space to reflect on the client and the counselling process.

- *Hypothetical questions*: a hypothetical or 'what if?' question is an effective way of challenging supervisees to see things from a different perspective or reflect on the consequences of their interventions, for example: *I understand your fears surrounding trust in your relationship with this client, and I'm wondering what might be the consequences if you don't disclose that your client is abusing their child.* Asking supervisees to think through the consequences of their actions can often serve as a helpful and non-blaming approach to challenge.

- *Information sharing*: using information in supervision can be a really positive way to challenge, for example: *Shall we see what the organisation's policy says about breaking confidentiality in cases like this?* It becomes the role of the information to offer the challenge and the supervisor's task is to assist the interpretation of the information, and support the supervisee to respond appropriately to what they have discovered.

Immediacy

The skill of immediacy, like challenge, is an advanced counselling skill that can challenge clients or supervisees to develop higher levels of self-awareness and recognise, explore and 'own' their emotional responses. Put simply, immediacy focuses on the 'here and now' in supervision. It attends to what is happening in the room between supervisor and supervisee and it requires the supervisor to bring themselves fully into the interaction. In the case study below, Hasan, the supervisor, is using immediacy with Julie, his supervisee.

Case study 8.2 Hasan and Julie

Julie (counsellor): *So that's it really. I seem to be getting nowhere with this client. We're just going round and round in circles. It's so frustrating, almost painful.*
Hasan (supervisor): *And how does it feel . . . bringing this client to supervision week after week?*
Julie: *It's driving me nuts!*

> Hasan: *It's driving you nuts . . . but as well as the frustration I'm getting the feeling that something else is going on for you too?*
>
> Julie: *What do you mean?*
>
> Hasan: *Well . . . you mention feeling fed up with the lack of progress, but I sense you are experiencing other feelings in relation to this piece of work . . .*
>
> Julie: *Well, obviously I feel like crap! Well, you would, wouldn't you if you spend week after week going over the same old thing?*
>
> Hasan: *It's tough when we can't 'fix' our clients, isn't it? So I guess I should be feeling like crap too every time you bring this client to supervision because I don't have the answers for you either? But actually, what I get more is the despair and 'stuck-ness' that this client is experiencing. It seems to me that you are sticking with this and containing your client's pain very effectively week after week until she is ready to move on. So . . . let's try to focus on your own and your client's feelings of being immobilised. What is stopping you both from making progress?*

In Case study 8.2 Hasan uses immediacy to challenge Julie to express her feelings and explore them more deeply. He also makes a helpful reference to the parallel process by pointing out that what is happening in supervision reflects the themes evident in counselling. Like challenge, immediacy is not easy. It often requires a 'deep breath' and should always come from a reflexive place. Asking someone to express emotions that they are working hard to ignore or suppress can be demanding and requires great care, a tentative approach, sensitivity and skill.

ACTIVITY 8.4

Let us return to the four scenarios introduced earlier in this chapter. Having digested what has been said about the activities of prescribing and feeding back and the skills of challenge and immediacy, would you change any of your initial responses? See below for suggestions about how to challenge in each case. Can you identify the category of intervention being used in each case (Heron, 1975)? And how effectively is the feedback given? Finally, can you spot the skills of challenge and immediacy in use in the examples below?

1. Your supervisee discloses that she has arranged to meet socially a client with whom she has recently ended a counselling relationship

There is a part of me that feels uncomfortable about what you have just told me. I wonder what my discomfort is all about? What questions might be going around in my head?

2. Your supervisee tells you that he has given money on a number of occasions to a young client who is destitute.

I'm asking myself the question: 'How has this has come about?' I feel concerned that what has happened may raise issues of dependency in the future. But before we talk about that, I think we need to check what the agency's policy has to say about offering gifts or money to clients.

3. Your supervisee discloses that he has known for some time that there is an issue of ongoing domestic violence with a couple he is counselling who have young children.

It's always difficult when we're working with clients where there is violence and children in the home. What have the couple told you about their violent behaviour in relation to the children? What would you do if they disclosed that they had been violent towards their children?

4. Your supervisee has given his phone number to a client who is suicidal. This goes against the policy of the organisation that employs him as a counsellor.

It's difficult when we find ourselves working with people in such desperate circumstances. I sense that you are feeling responsible for this client's life. Let's talk about that further in a moment. But first, we need to be clear that this organisation does not allow counsellors to give their private phone numbers to clients. There is a hotline number that clients can call after hours that provides a link to Samaritans in circumstances such as these.

The working alliance stage of the relationship is not all about challenging. What is clear, though, is that the relationship at this point should be sufficiently robust to enable the supervisor to prescribe, feed back, and use challenge and immediacy constructively in order to develop best practice. Of course, supervision and the supervisory relationship will be reviewed regularly (this will be examined in Chapter 9), and issues including style of challenge and feedback can be discussed fully. Both supervisor and supervisee have the opportunity to share their perceptions of what is working in the relationship, what is helpful and what might be developed further.

So far in this study of the development of the supervisory relationship through each of its stages from 'preparing' to the 'working alliance', we have focused on supervision delivered in individual interactions. Furthermore, the focus thus far has been on a straightforward dialogue between supervisor and supervisee. This is not surprising: supervision, for the most part, like the counselling relationship, generally involves two people sitting in a room and talking together. There is a risk, though, that opportunities to gain greater insight, understanding, reflection and self-knowledge are missed by not engaging with more creative approaches to the work. In addition, introducing creative methods in supervision can also encourage their use in counselling: the parallel process. And for some clients (and supervisees, for that matter), who may find it difficult to express themselves in words, taking an alternative, creative approach can be liberating.

CREATIVE METHODS IN SUPERVISION

Exploring new methodologies and experiencing different ways of working together may at first feel unsafe for both the supervisor and supervisee, but there is much to be gained from it.

(Schuck and Wood, 2011, p15)

As the quote above suggests, moving outside the comfort zone of tried and trusted ways of working can be daunting, but ultimately rewarding. It is helpful to remind ourselves that play is an important element of learning. Thinking back to childhood, most of our learning experiences develop through play or taking part in creative activities. As adults, though, we are often resistant to exploring feelings, ideas and concepts creatively, possibly as a response to comments we received about our creative endeavours when we were younger. Supervisees may feel exposed when invited to work in more creative ways in supervision, experiencing feelings of ineptitude or possibly fearing ridicule. Schuck and Wood recognise this anxiety and suggest seven steps to introduce effective creative working.

- Develop a clear contract with supervisee/s: ensure that ground rules are discussed and agreement about participation is reached.

- Set up a conducive environment: ensure that the props, activities and resources required for the activity are accessible and sufficient.

- Give supervisee/s time, space and quiet to engage with the activities: working creatively invites supervisees to access deep emotions, thoughts and feelings.

- Observe and offer constructive feedback: the supervisor's role is not that of clairvoyant or mystic, interpreting what has been produced by the supervisee, but rather one of facilitator, feeding back observations on the process.

- Encourage discussion, critical analysis and action planning: engage supervisee/s in a discussion relating to their learning. How might the new insights inform their future practice?

- Encourage deeper reflection through the use of journals or reflective diaries: suggest that supervisee/s make notes or take pictures of their work during the session to enable insight through reflection following the session.

- Debrief fully: if role play is used, ensure that supervisees come out of role fully. Allow time to discuss how they have been left feeling as a result of the activity.

REFLECTION POINT

List your instinctive response to using creative methods in supervision. Don't think about it too deeply – just jot down words that sum up how you might feel about engaging in role play, simulation, art work, drama and so on.

How you respond to the concept of creativity in both counselling and supervision is likely to depend on previous experiences you may have had. For example, if, like me, your artistic endeavours were criticised or, worse still, ridiculed as a child, you may find the thought of drawing a picture in supervision terrifying. On the other hand, if you embrace your creativity and like to express yourself through pictures, sounds, words or movement, you will feel excited by the opportunity to engage in creative activities in supervision. Whatever your initial response, take time to consider the five activities outlined below. How effectively might each promote deeper reflection and insight into practice? What might be the challenges of facilitating the activity? What impact might undertaking the activity have on the supervisory relationship?

- *Using artwork and visualisation*: visualisation can be used in two forms in supervision. Supervisees can be asked to undertake exploratory visualisation where they are invited to use resources such as pictures or stories to act as metaphors, prompting deep levels of reflection and 'freeing up' their minds to gain new perspectives; alternatively, supervisees can use visualisation to create their own metaphors and meaning, producing creative pieces to assist the process, whereby supervisees are invited to use a metaphor to describe someone they are working with. Some supervisees may struggle initially with this concept, so the activity can be simplified in the first instance by suggesting a metaphor. For example, I have asked supervisees to think about a client and draw them as a fish. I ask them the following questions: What does the fish look like, smell like, feel like, sound like and taste like? My role as supervisor is to encourage supervisees to explore the client with whom they are working by accessing all of their five senses. The object of the metaphor offers a safe space to reflect on the client and the relationship between client and supervisee.

- *Human sculpting*: this is a powerful activity that can be used in group supervision. Negotiate with the group for one supervisee to present a case using sculpt. The supervisee will assign 'roles' to various group members and these roles will represent a client and significant others in the client's world. The supervisee then 'places' the 'client' and their significant others in relation to each other. For example, the client may be placed in the middle of the group with the 'father' standing close by while the 'mother' is positioned at some distance. The supervisee will ask the participants to adopt a particular stance and expression, but otherwise the activity is completed in silence. Once all the characters are arranged, they are asked to hold the pose for some minutes and allow themselves to experience how it feels in their assigned character's 'skin.' After some moments each character is asked to feed back how they are feeling about themselves and their relationship to others in the sculpt. This can be a very powerful activity that offers real insight. It must be sensitively facilitated by the supervisor, and a full debrief should take place once sculpting has ended.

- *Using pebbles, shells and other objects and figures*: the use of objects and figures to facilitate in-depth understanding, like the sculpt activity above, can be very powerful. In brief, the supervisor provides objects for the supervisee to 'play' with and position. These objects could include a basket of different shaped pebbles or shells, a collection of toy figures, a jar of coloured buttons, small animal figures or even toy bricks. It is for the supervisee to use these resources and select a pebble, shell, figure and so on to represent their client and other characters who form part of the client's story. The work comes in the analysis of the symbols selected. *Why that pebble – big, flat and heavy? Why choose a lion as a symbol to represent the client's partner? How smooth and shiny that button is and what a vibrant colour! How close you have placed the elephant and the lamb figures. I wonder why?* The power of this activity cannot be overestimated. When I used this method with a client over several weeks, they asked to keep the small, round pebble they had chosen as their own symbol and often referred to 'keeping the pebble safe' in subsequent sessions.

- *Two-chair work*: the concept of the 'empty chair' or two-chair work originated in Gestalt therapy and can be used to great effect in one-to-one supervision. The supervisor invites the supervisee to talk to the empty chair, imagining their client is sitting there. Then the supervisee swaps places and sits in the 'client's' chair, responding to the empty 'supervisee's' chair as the client. A dialogue between supervisee and client is played out as the supervisee alternates between the two chairs. The experience of 'being' the client can elicit new insight and enable powerful responses. The role of the facilitator is to observe, feed back and engage the supervisee in an analysis of what has taken place.

- *Role play*: this activity can be used in a number of ways, for example, setting up a full role play activity in group supervision, or taking a few moments in one-to-one supervision to suggest to a supervisee that you, as supervisor, take on the role of the supervisee's client to 'try out' how different responses might feel. The experience of role play can be powerful and, as in the group sculpt, the importance of effective debriefing should not be underestimated.

REFLECTION POINT

Which of the activities above would you be willing to use in supervision? What might the activity achieve? What resistance might a supervisor encounter when they suggest this activity and how might this be overcome?

What is presented above is a 'snapshot' of a range of activities that can be used effectively to explore client work, develop greater self-awareness and deepen the working alliance in the supervision process. Working creatively is not confined to the working alliance stage of the relationship, but a level of trust in the supervisory relationship must exist in order for supervisees to feel safe enough to 'take the risk' of trying something new while discovering and exposing elements of themselves that they may previously have kept hidden (Luft, 1984).

STAGE FOUR: MAINTAINING A WORKING ALLIANCE

ACTIVITY 8.5

This chapter has focused on the working alliance stage of the development of the supervisory relationship. Let us return to our three supervision couples: Mark and Bridget, Fran and Gemma, and Karen and Clive. How far has the working alliance stage been achieved?

Case study 8.3 Mark and Bridget

Mark has now met with Bridget for supervision on twelve occasions. In the last session together they undertook a Gestalt activity where Mark suggested that Bridget use the two-chairs technique to 'talk to' a counselling client with whom she was struggling. As she explained to Mark, she felt as though she had come to a 'full stop' with the work. Although Mark had reservations about how Bridget might respond to his suggestion, he was confident enough in their relationship to invite Bridget to try out a more creative technique. During the session, Bridget, who had not participated in this type of activity before, became overwhelmed by powerful feelings of rejection and loss, which, when discussed, provided her with some clues and strategies for progressing her work with this client. Mark asked Bridget to reflect on how she had felt about undertaking this activity and identify what she had learned. From that discussion, Bridget was able to share how much she valued Mark as a supervisor; particularly now he was challenging her to consider different perspectives and work in new and innovative ways.

Case study 8.4 Fran and Gemma

Fran has met with her supervisee Gemma on twelve occasions. As this is Gemma's first experience of supervision (and counselling), Fran is pleased with her supervisee's progress. They have discussed in depth the purpose of supervision and have reflected on their relationship, which has included airing the issues of dependency and transference. Gemma is beginning to work more autonomously and use the supervision sessions in a positive way, bringing clients and focusing in more detail on their issues rather than their stories. Fran is excited by Gemma's development but is conscious that Gemma's newfound confidence in her practice is fragile. This was illustrated last week, as Gemma burst into tears when Fran challenged her to reflect on an aspect of her work with a client who was self-harming. Gemma appeared to regress to a previous point in their relationship where she constantly stated *I'm getting it wrong aren't I?* This led Fran to reflect on both the nature and efficacy of her challenge and the development of the supervisory relationship. She acknowledged that it might be some time before the working alliance phase is reached, as there are still issues of trust and confidence-building between them.

Case study 8.5 Karen and Clive

Karen and Clive have met together on twenty occasions. In the last few weeks Karen has used the skill of immediacy to invite Clive to reflect in more depth, on his own responses in relation to his counselling practice. In the last session, as Clive was presenting a client, Karen stopped him and said: *As you're talking about this client I feel at a distance somehow. It's like I'm watching a film or TV drama. What*

I feel I'm missing is where you fit into this piece of work. What are your feelings, what is your emotional response to this client? This intervention led to a revealing discussion where Clive expressed his difficulty throughout his counsellor training, supervision and his own personal therapy with talking about his intimate thoughts and feelings. He covered this revelation by joking that he had got away with it so far. And Karen responded by asking: I wonder what it is that you think you have got away with? What is it you fear? As Clive left the session he turned to Karen and said: I wasn't sure that this would work out at the start. Our approaches to counselling come from quite different places, yours being psychodynamic and mine being CBT, and I didn't know how this would be in supervision. But it has been enlightening. I've been a counsellor for five years, but this is the first time that I think I've really understood what supervision is all about. Thank you.

Clearly, each supervision relationship has progressed. In the case of Mark and Bridget, the difficulties around challenge that were evident when we observed the couple in the last chapter have been addressed. Furthermore, Mark is inviting Bridget to engage in more creative activities in supervision and Bridget is responding positively to this. The supervisory relationship contains strong elements of the working alliance stage whereby trust, openness, vulnerability and risk-taking are evident.

In the case of Fran and Gemma, Gemma's inexperience and newness in the role of both counsellor and supervisee has had an impact. Although Fran is observing higher levels of autonomy in Gemma's approach to her practice and supervision, there is still difficulty in Gemma being able to hear and accept feedback and challenge as a positive aspect of learning. Fran is aware that their relationship needs to develop to a level of openness that will enable Gemma to trust herself as a counsellor and feel safe enough to respond positively to constructive criticism.

For Karen and Clive the working alliance stage has been reached. This is evident by the complex and risky personal disclosure Clive made in his last supervision session. It is interesting to note that the difference in their counselling orientations has not acted as the barrier that both parties feared at the outset. In Chapter 9 we will return to these supervisory relationships at a point where the relationship in each case has come to an end.

CHAPTER SUMMARY

This chapter established the characteristics of the working alliance stage of the supervisory relationship. It explored:

- the features of the working alliance stage – honesty, openness, self-disclosure, risk-taking and so on;

- the tasks of prescribing and giving feedback, key to ensuring the normative function of supervision;

- the use of the advanced skills of challenge and immediacy in supervision;

- the part that creativity can play in deepening understanding about client work and developing the supervisory relationship.

It is important to note at this point that some supervisory relationships may not reach the working alliance stage. That does not mean that they have failed, but rather that the climate may not have provided the necessary conditions for the relationship to flourish. In some cases circumstances dictate that not enough time is available for the relationship to develop to this deeper level before it terminates. The termination of the supervisory relationship will be explored in the next chapter.

SUGGESTED FURTHER READING

Schuck, C and Wood, J (2011) *Inspiring creative supervision.* London: Jessica Kingsley.

A wonderful resource that includes suggestions for using creative methods in both one-to-one and group supervision.

Shohet, R (ed.) (2011) *Supervision as transformation: A passion for learning.* London: Jessica Kingsley.

Includes personal reflections, case studies and shared experiences of building transformative supervisory relationships in a range of contexts.

CHAPTER 9

Moving on – ending the supervisory relationship

Jane Westergaard

CORE KNOWLEDGE

This chapter will provide the opportunity to:

- establish the purpose of review in the supervisory relationship;
- reflect on the meaning of 'endings' in supervision;
- consider how to manage endings in the supervisory relationship effectively;
- explore the concept of 'new beginnings'.

INTRODUCTION

The only thing that both supervisor and supervisee know with any certainty at the start of a supervisory relationship is that it will, at some point, come to an end. This might happen after one session, ten sessions or ten years of working together, but ultimately the relationship will run its course, and an ending, planned or unplanned, will take place. Counsellors are familiar with the concept of 'endings' in client work, and this will have been explored in depth as part of their counselling training. They will know that endings can be very personal and highly emotional, for both client and counsellor, bringing, as they often do, past experiences and losses to the fore.

Although much has been written about termination in counselling (Mander, 2000; Murdin, 2000; Davis, 2008; Dryden, 2008; Nelson-Jones, 2012), there is little to draw on in the literature that relates specifically to the process of ending in supervision. In her book on counselling supervision in organisations, Copeland (2005) devotes a chapter to ending the supervisory relationship, and she makes some helpful practical suggestions about strategies for managing endings effectively. But the dearth of available literature should not suggest that endings in supervision are insignificant events. They are not.

This chapter completes our investigation of the stages of development of the supervisory relationship: from preparing for supervision, through establishing and progressing the supervisory relationship, achieving a working alliance and here, finally, ending the relationship between supervisor and supervisee. The chapter begins by considering how and when supervision should be reviewed, before going on to define what is meant by 'ending', to explore how and why the relationship might come to an end, to establish attendant feelings and responses and to consider how to manage endings effectively in supervision. The concept of an ending as a 'new beginning' is also discussed. Finally, we return to our three supervisory relationships to see how effectively the relationship reaches a conclusion in each case.

REVIEWING SUPERVISION

It is important at the outset to be clear about what is meant by review here. Review as it is discussed in this chapter does not refer specifically to the activity of making judgements, feeding back and reporting on the proficiency of the supervisee's practice; this has been dealt with in earlier chapters. Rather, it pertains to the process of supervision, reviewing the relationship as it progresses over time, paying attention to any issues and problems that require resolution or positive aspects that are working well and could be developed further.

Sterner (2009) researched the impact of the supervisory relationship on a range of aspects of counselling practice. One of the most significant findings was the correlation between the effectiveness of the relationship between supervisor and supervisee (the quality of the working alliance) and reduced stress and burnout experienced by supervisees in their counselling practice. If we are to accept the powerful role that supervision can play in supporting and improving different elements relating to the work of counsellors, it is important that time is spent in making sure that the supervisory relationship develops effectively and is optimised. Like many aspects of supervision, the activity of review between supervisor and supervisee parallels the counselling process. Review of the ongoing relationship between counsellor and client and evaluation of its effectiveness when the relationship comes to an end are activities central to counselling practice. Counsellors will be aware of the importance of regularly reviewing or 'checking out' how they and their client feel that the work and the relationship between them is progressing so the concept of review will not be new.

ACTIVITY 9.1

Take a moment to reflect on both your counselling and your supervision relationships and note down your answers to the questions below. Compare your answers with the responses from Calvin, an experienced supervisor, in Case study 9.1.

- How regularly do you review the relationship and the process?

- What questions are asked in order to facilitate an effective review?

- What does the review achieve?

- What difficulties or issues have you experienced in reviewing the relationship?

These questions were put to an experienced supervisor, Calvin, whose experiences can be seen in Case study 9.1.

Case study 9.1 Calvin: supervisor

Actually, I think that I probably review supervision with my supervisees every time we meet, to a certain extent. For example, we 'check in' at the start of each session, and I always ask how the supervisee is feeling at the end too. I hope that I'm able to pick up if something has happened in a session that has raised issues about supervision for the supervisee or for me, for that matter, and I'd use immediacy to prompt reflection and share my concerns. But I also undertake more formal reviews. It pretty much works like it does in my counselling practice, in that I suggest at the start that we meet for six sessions and on the sixth session we take time to review how the relationship is developing. If it feels necessary – like if I'm working with a new or trainee counsellor – I might continue to do regular reviews every six sessions or so. If I'm working with an experienced counsellor, I may review less frequently, maybe every six months, or even once a year in some cases. It's important for me to be clear with my supervisees about how these reviews are recorded and how they may be different from other, more formal reviews and reports on practice, particularly in the case of trainee counsellors.

Where we arrange a review I suggest – in the session before the review is due to take place – that they reflect on the supervision process before we next meet and come ready to share thoughts, feelings and feedback. In the review itself, we focus our discussions on what happens in supervision that works well, what isn't so effective and what could be developed further. I ask the supervisee what it is that I do in supervision that they find helpful and what they find less helpful. I share my observations of the ways in which my supervisee engages with both the work and the supervision process, and I ask them to do the same.

> *The review ensures that the relationship between us is continuing to develop effectively and that the supervisee is making good use of the process, and I'm doing everything I can to facilitate and support them. It highlights areas of the counsellor's practice and supervision that are working well and it seeks to identify and reflect on how we work on issues that need development. In most cases the review is a really positive experience for both of us. I see it as a time to celebrate the work the counsellor is doing with clients and to ensure that supervision is continuing to be an integral part of that process.*
>
> *Of course, there are times when the review throws up challenges – either for me or for the supervisee. On one occasion I felt it necessary to feed back my concerns about my supervisee's commitment to supervision – she often arrived late or didn't turn up at all. On another occasion I'd become aware that I was increasingly taking on the role of teacher or 'expert' in supervision and I wanted to raise this in the review and seek my supervisee's perspective about what appeared to be happening between us. Once, my supervisee expressed the view that reviewing supervision was taking up valuable time that could have been used to discuss client work. In this case I asked my supervisee what he would say to a client who questioned the value of reviewing the effectiveness of counselling. This helped to open up the discussion between us, and actually served to strengthen our relationship.*

The point concerning the parallel process is important. As already stated, counsellors identify 'review' as central to their client practice. It helps to keep the relationship focused and ensure that goals about the work are shared and understood between counsellor and client. The same applies to supervision. Regular review provides a forum to focus on the 'here and now' of supervision rather than the 'there and then' of client work. It addresses key modes contained in Hawkins and Shohet's (2006) seven-eyed process model (see Chapters 3 and 7 for a fuller explanation), including the supervisee, the supervisor and, in particular, the supervisory relationship. These 'eyes' form the focus of review, and if review sessions are not formalised as part of the process, these modes may become neglected.

Where review is effective the following outcomes should be achieved.

- Greater levels of trust, openness and honesty in the relationship.

- A clear sense of what is working well in supervision and what needs to be done differently in order to make supervision more effective.

- An opportunity to introduce, explore and try out new and more creative ways of working in supervision in the future.

- Deeper levels of both reflection and reflexivity on the part of both supervisor and supervisee, examining their own thoughts and feelings in relation to the other.

- The addressing of any problems/issues in the relationship, making alternative arrangements if necessary (for example, a change of supervisor).

REFLECTION POINT

Focus on a recent supervisory relationship – either as supervisor or supervisee.

- How was the review process carried out?

- What are the positives that have come out of the review process for you?

- What was done well?

- If you feel that you have not had the opportunity yet to review the relationship, what kind of issues would you like to raise when the review session takes place?

As explained at the outset, review is not an activity that should be consigned only to the ending phase of the supervisory relationship (although, of course, review and evaluation are important when any helping relationship comes to a close). Nor is it something that happens purely as a response to requirements from training providers or for accreditation. Rather, care should be taken to understand review throughout supervision as a process that is central to the effective building of the relationship. And, when done well, review in supervision can and should lead to greater shared personal and professional insight.

Having established the importance of review throughout the supervision process, we can move to examine in more detail the principles for ending the supervisory relationship effectively. As I write this, I am aware of my own hesitation. And this hesitation, I believe, exemplifies the complexity and challenge of 'endings'. The word itself, when spoken or read, will inevitably strike a chord with everyone. Done well, an ending (in any context – not only supervision) can achieve 'closure', a positive resolution that results in feelings of sadness, perhaps, but also warmth, achievement, celebration, well-being, forgiveness (if appropriate) and understanding. Often, though, endings are not managed effectively. They might be sudden, unexpected or traumatic, and may induce feelings of loss, pain, anger, abandonment, isolation, loneliness or even despair. It is almost impossible to reflect on current endings without summoning images of past separations – positive or negative – that have left a lasting impression. And endings are not always straightforward. They can be messy, incomplete, unresolved or even violent. No wonder I'm hesitating! But ending is as central to supervision as it is to counselling, and it is therefore the responsibility of this book about supervision to tackle the subject. Furthermore, it is worth noting that the title of this chapter is 'Moving on – ending the supervisory relationship', suggesting that 'ending' is fundamental to 'moving on', and 'moving on' implies a positive response. In addition, moving on is crucial to our own personal and professional development as both counsellors and supervisors.

ENDINGS IN SUPERVISION

Carroll (1996) suggests that 'terminating' supervision is generally a planned activity whereby both supervisor and supervisee know that the relationship will be coming to an end, and have the opportunity to work towards making the ending a positive experience. This is certainly true in most cases – but not all. In addition, even where an ending is planned and worked towards, it does not necessarily take away the attendant feelings and emotional responses evoked by the separation. Wall (1994) highlights the parallel process here, suggesting that supervisees will have worked with endings in their counselling practice with clients and will have brought these experiences to supervision. Supervisors will therefore already be aware of the ways that their supervisees experience and manage endings. They should then be well placed to assess how to facilitate the termination when it occurs in supervision. Furthermore, because both supervisor and supervisee, in their roles as counsellors, will have experienced endings with clients, both planned and unplanned, they will already be familiar with their own range of responses to ending a professional helping relationship. Let us start this examination of endings in supervision by reflecting on the range of feelings and responses that termination can provoke.

ACTIVITY 9.2

Take a moment to consider your own response to endings. Look at the list below and reflect on your life experiences thus far to identify the following.

- A professional ending (for example, leaving a job, training programme, education, personal therapy or supervision).

- A personal ending (for example, the end of a relationship with a family member, partner or good friend).

- A planned ending (for example, finishing a programme of study, leaving school, moving to a new area or ending with a client in counselling).

- An unplanned ending (for example, an unexpected bereavement or a client who simply stopped coming to counselling).

Now make a list of the feelings that dominated at the time and reflect on how effectively you managed the ending in each case.

- How, if at all, did you achieve 'closure'?

- What is your response now when you reflect on each ending? What feelings were generated at the time? What feelings are you left with?

- How do you think each ending has had an impact on subsequent endings in your life?

This is a challenging activity, and not one to which I can offer guidance, insight or interpretation. Each of our individual responses will be informed by our experiences of endings, terminations or loss throughout our lives – both positive and negative. Some of these endings may have engendered feelings of intense relief, celebration, anticipation or excitement. Others will have left a warm and hazy glow in their wake. However, some endings are likely to have provoked less pleasant feelings, including loss, sadness, anger, grief, guilt, self-doubt and despair.

There is a range of personal responses to painful endings, and we may not always react in the same way. Some may experience the feelings 'head-on', immersed in, but able to express their grief and loss, while others may respond to the intensity by running away and hiding, protecting themselves from emotions that they may find overwhelming. We may deny painful feelings about endings when they occur, only to find ourselves experiencing strong emotional responses to what seem to be less significant losses later in life. Others may experience intense anger or rage at their loss, while some may feel overwhelming despair and lethargy. Some may find positive and proactive ways to deal with their loss, particularly in the case of sudden or unexplained death through illness, accident or as a victim of crime, where the bereaved become involved actively in campaigning or charity activities. Our background, gender, ethnicity, culture, beliefs and so on are also likely to play a part in informing our responses to endings. For example, young boys often receive messages about the need to 'be brave' or 'not cry' when endings occur. This can influence their responses to loss in later life (d'Ardenne and Mahtani, 1989).

The list above highlights examples of responses to endings that happen *to* us, influenced by external factors, but it is possible to experience changes that signify endings that take place *within* us, too. For example, we have all become adults, and therefore our childhood has come to an end. Our bodies alter as we get older, and we have to accept that these changes may have an impact on elements of our lives – for example, our ability to run for a bus, hear clearly in a crowd or see what we are reading in focus may all be impaired. As you are reading, if you have experienced one or more of these losses, you may reflect on how you have managed each transition. You might also find yourself acknowledging that, alongside the sadness, there are often positive aspects that can accompany a change.

What we have clarified so far is that endings are likely to prompt emotional responses. Even planned or desired endings can provoke strong feelings, both positive and negative. So an ending in supervision, as in counselling, should acknowledge the significance of the relationship and the feelings of both parties in order that a termination is managed and closure is achieved. Before we examine how endings can be carried out effectively in supervision, it is helpful to identify the reasons that supervision might come to an end. In an ideal world, of course, the ending of the relationship will be planned. But this is not always the case.

Writing about planned endings in counselling, Horton (2012) describes five areas that should be explored when it is known that counselling is reaching an end. These are:

- focusing on what the counselling has achieved;
- identifying what still needs to be developed/worked on;
- examining how change and development has taken place;
- considering what might happen in the future;
- reflecting on the nature of the counsellor/client relationship.

Below, Calvin, the supervisor who shared his approach to reviewing supervision earlier in this chapter, goes on to explore how he manages a planned ending in supervision. Bearing in mind the parallel process, to what extent are the five areas identified above as best practice for endings in counselling present in Calvin's supervision practice?

Case study 9.2 Calvin: supervisor

I've been lucky as I have only ever experienced one unplanned ending in supervision. All the rest of my endings with supervisees have been planned. That means we can prepare ourselves for what is about to happen, acknowledge how we feel about ending, identify the progress that has been made, celebrate the supervisee's achievements, reflect on our relationship and plan for the next phase of the supervisee's development.

*   When I think about it, I realise that I make a point of mentioning 'endings' in our very first session together. For me, it's an important part of the contracting phase, whereby I explain that I will give my supervisee as much notice as I can about the ending of the relationship; and I ask my supervisee, wherever possible, to do the same. This means that the ending should not happen quickly, without preparation, and should certainly not come as an abrupt termination.*

So, when I know that the relationship is coming to an end, for example, if I've changed jobs, I've informed my supervisees as soon as I know. This means that ideally we have at least two or three sessions together before our final meeting. I would start the session by saying that I have some news to share and would reassure my supervisee that we will have plenty of time to talk about this in subsequent sessions. We always have some space, there and then, to acknowledge the immediate response. Even where an ending is planned, it may still come as a shock when it is first mentioned.

In subsequent sessions we talk about our supervision and the impact it has had on the supervisee's counselling practice. I ask supervisees to reflect on where they were at the start of the process and to identify where they are now. Sometimes we use creative techniques to do this. For example, one supervisee chose to write a letter to her inexperienced self at the start of supervision, from herself now, as an experienced counsellor having attended supervision for three years. She found this to be a powerful and enlightening activity.

Often supervisees make the link between their own experience of ending supervision and what it must be like for clients to come to the end in counselling. If the supervisee does not make this observation, I offer it to them.

The ending of supervision, perhaps more than at any other time, provides an opportunity for me to share my own feelings with my supervisees. Supervision is a learning process, and often I will be amazed at how much I've learned by working with a supervisee. I will always share this, acknowledging the contribution that the supervisee has made to developing my knowledge and understanding.

Sometimes supervisees offer cards or small gifts at our last session together. I accept these with thanks, but I choose not to give presents to supervisees on ending. Most importantly, we talk about the notion of ending as a new start, a new phase in our lives and I help supervisees to reflect on their next steps and what they want to achieve further in their counselling practice.

It's hard, but I try to avoid 'see you later' type comments that serve to minimise the impact of endings. It is interesting that I have never bumped into any of my supervisees again once the relationship has ended, and therefore to say 'see you soon' would be dishonest.

It should come as no surprise to find that Calvin's reflections adhere to Horton's five areas identified above. By now, the significance of the parallel process should be firmly embedded with readers. In summary, then, an ending should:

- be discussed at the beginning, in the contracting stage of supervision (some organisations time-limit supervision with the same supervisor, and this should be made clear at the outset);
- be shared with the supervisee/supervisor at the earliest possible point, ideally with at least two or three supervision sessions remaining;

- allow time to acknowledge the feelings of both supervisor and supervisee;
- reflect on the parallel process in counselling;
- provide an opportunity to reflect on the developments the supervisee has made;
- celebrate achievements;
- focus on and evaluate the supervisory relationship;
- provide an opportunity to plan for the future;
- clarify the nature of any continuing relationship (for example, if supervisor and supervisee continue to have contact as colleagues in the same organisation, but not as supervisor and supervisee).

If the points above are addressed, then there is every chance that the relationship will end on a positive note, and both parties, although left with feelings of sadness, will also experience hope and anticipation concerning the future.

So far we have focused on planned endings, but you will know from your response to the previous activity that managing and responding to unplanned endings can prove more problematic. Supervisees will be aware of the challenge of managing unplanned endings from their counselling practice. Most counsellors at some point in their practice experience the frustration, disappointment, self-doubt and confusion generated by the client who simply terminates the relationship without explanation or warning. Horton explains:

> *Incomplete ending by default can haunt therapists for some time. It's all too easy to slip into imagining all sorts of circumstances or reasons, including the therapist's own mistakes or incompetence, for clients failing to attend to the end of a negotiated contract or agreed period of therapy.*

> (Horton, 2012, p128)

Unlike counselling relationships, which often end this way, particularly in the case of counselling children and young people (Kazdin, 1996), it is highly unlikely that a supervision relationship will terminate without some indication of what has happened. It would be very unusual for a counsellor or supervisor to simply disappear, leaving the other to dwell on a list of increasingly traumatic or fanciful hypothetical scenarios. Where a counselling agency, training provider or professional organisation is involved, it is likely that the reasons for leaving will have been made clear to someone. In this case the practice manager, tutor or colleague in the organisation can pass on information about why the supervisor or supervisee is unable to continue the supervisory relationship. In private practice, it is, perhaps, more difficult for either supervisee or supervisor to 'follow up' their colleague in the event of an unplanned termination.

An unplanned ending in supervision can generate feelings of confusion, inadequacy, hurt, pain, rejection, abandonment or anger – for both supervisor and supervisee. An understanding of the reasons why the relationship has terminated can help to ameliorate the painful emotions experienced. Of course, if we know our supervisor has been involved in an accident, we will still be left feeling shocked and sad, but we will also understand that what has happened was not our fault. We have not done something wrong, been rejected, caused something bad to happen. In the case of an unplanned ending due to the supervisor leaving, supervisees who are in training or employed should be offered alternative supervision by their organisation without delay. This will help them to work through the feelings they are experiencing as a result of the loss. If this situation occurs in private practice, the supervisee will need to make contact with a new supervisor as a matter of urgency.

Before we move on and reflect on the ways in which our three supervision couples are experiencing the ending of their relationships, let us take a moment to reflect further about the concept of an ending as a new beginning.

MOVING ON

The notion of 'ending' at first glance appears to suggest finality. There is often a sense that an ending provides a full stop, a point at which we can go no further. Of course, this is not the case. Without wishing to sound morbid, apart from the ultimate ending – our own death – we continue to function after endings have taken place, however painful or traumatic they have been. Those with strongly held religious beliefs would argue that even our death does not signify an ending, but simply means that we pass on to the next stage of our journey.

The ending of a supervisory relationship, as we have already established, provides the opportunity to reflect on what we have learned and consider what it is that we would like to continue to work on and develop in our professional practice. As part of a reflective learning process, ending is central to developing, moving on and changing, and our experience and our learning are presented as cyclical rather than linear. For many of us, the process of supervision can, to a large extent, be viewed as a cycle. The supervisory relationship model introduced in this book could also be represented as an ongoing process whereby we prepare for, establish, progress, reach the working alliance and then end one supervisory relationship before moving on to preparing for the next. Most counsellors will work with more than one supervisor: a supervisor identified while on placement in training, a new supervisor once qualified if working for a different agency or organisation and different supervisors throughout their counselling career.

Each ending (and new beginning) will be a unique experience – as it is in counselling with clients. As part of the ending process, supervisees should be encouraged to think about their next steps and make plans for these. It may be that a supervisee will be starting with a new supervisor, or taking a break from counselling or leaving altogether. Whatever the circumstance, the process of ending supervision involves identifying and considering the next step, the moving on, the new beginning.

Schuck and Wood (2011) suggest some excellent creative activities for supervision that attend to the 'moving on' aspect of ending. For example, in individual supervision they encourage supervisees to engage in a closing ceremony whereby a moment is taken to reflect, breathe deeply and think about what they want to say or do to make the ending complete – before they move on to the next step in their professional development. They also suggest that both supervisor and supervisee should make a list detailing positive elements they have appreciated in each other and expressing their hopes for the future. The ending for a group in supervision provides more opportunities to celebrate, using creative methods. Of course, in the case of group supervision there is an added complication in that group members are saying goodbye to more than just their supervisor; they are finishing a relationship with the group itself.

STAGE FIVE: ENDING THE SUPERVISORY RELATIONSHIP

ACTIVITY 9.3

Having focused on ending and moving on in this chapter, let us return to the three supervisory relationships we have followed through the supervision process. As you read, consider the following questions.

- How effectively is the ending managed in each case?

- What feelings are both supervisor and supervisee left with?

- How effectively does the final session prepare the supervisee for the next steps?

Case study 9.3 Mark and Bridget

Mark and his supervisee Bridget have worked together for three years. They have engaged in positive and fruitful supervision and have reached the working alliance stage of their relationship. Initial issues concerning challenge between them have been resolved and they are both using supervision much more creatively in order to examine, reflect on and develop practice. Both Mark and Bridget have been informed by the counselling agency for which they work that the policy on supervision has changed, and no supervisor can now work with the same supervisee for more than three years. A letter is sent by the agency to all counsellors and supervisors to inform them of this decision. At their first meeting following receipt of the letter, Mark asks Bridget how she feels about the change and the fact that they will only have three more sessions together. The agency decision for both parties was unexpected. Bridget expressed her anger and frustration, and Mark shared his feelings of sadness that their relationship would be coming to an end. Together, they planned how they would manage the process of termination in the next few sessions. They agreed to devote their final session together to reviewing, evaluating and ending their relationship. At this final session, they undertook a creative activity whereby Bridget decided to draw a 'shield', which represented her learning through supervision. The shield was divided into four quarters: my learning; my future; my experience of supervision; my motto. Bridget used images and words to complete her shield, and she shared this with Mark, who asked if he could add his own reflections. Together they acknowledged their feelings of sadness that the relationship had come to an end, but they each shared their hopes for the future too. Bridget ended the session by folding the shield up and taking it with her, thanking Mark for all his help and support as she did so. Mark responded by asking Bridget for a hug before she left the room. They parted with a smile and a wave.

Case study 9.4 Fran and Gemma

Fran has been working with trainee counsellor Gemma for six months while Gemma has been on placement at the local college, but Gemma is now in the final term of her placement. She arrived late for her fifteenth supervision session with Fran, slumped in the chair and appeared to be upset. Fran began by using immediacy to reflect on Gemma's demeanour. Gemma burst into tears and explained that she had made the decision that counselling was not for her – at least, not at this point in her life – and that she wanted to quit her training and her placement. She explained that she hadn't wanted to come to this session as she couldn't see the point, but her tutor on the counselling course and her placement manager had suggested that she should. Fran was shocked, but, on reflection, not surprised by Gemma's decision. She had sensed Gemma's lack of confidence in her counselling practice and although she appeared to be making progress, Gemma had experienced something of a 'wobble' recently. Fran asked Gemma how she would like to use her final supervision session. Gemma said she didn't care how they used it – as long as they didn't talk about why she had made the decision to end counselling, as she'd talked to both her tutor and placement manager about her decision at some length and felt 'worn out' by it. Fran suggested that they spend some time reflecting on how the process of supervision and their supervisory relationship had had an impact on Gemma – in terms of her counselling practice but also in relation to the decision she had made to leave counselling. Gemma agreed, but Fran sensed her reluctance, and Gemma's responses continued to be monosyllabic. Fran used immediacy again, suggesting that Gemma did not feel 'present' in the session and asking again how she would like to use the rest of the time they had together. Gemma responded by reaching for her coat, getting up out of her chair and turning to the door, saying *I just want to go. Thank you.* Fran was left with the sight of Gemma's back as she slammed the door behind her.

Case study 9.5 Karen and Clive

Karen has been supervising Clive for five years. Their relationship has been at the working alliance phase for some time and Karen has been delighted by the way in which Clive has developed as a much more reflexive counsellor. Where in their early sessions he found it difficult to engage in any exploration of his own feelings and responses in relation to his client work, he has now 'opened up' and developed high levels of self-awareness and self-knowledge. Clive has put this change down, in large part, to his supervisor. He believes that Karen's psycho-dynamic approach, although challenging at first, has helped him to develop as a counsellor and a human being. Karen, too, has learned much about CBT and the approaches Clive uses with his clients in order to effect change, and she has been surprised and delighted by what he has achieved in his client practice.

Early in the relationship, when the contract was agreed, Karen had explained that she works with supervisees for a maximum of five years. Six months ago, it was agreed that a supervision session be set aside for review. During this session, Karen raised the issue of the relationship coming to an end as the five years was nearly up. Clive tried to persuade Karen to continue as his supervisor, but Karen explained that she felt it was important for both of them to adhere to the contract they'd made together and 'move on'. Since that meeting, the subject of ending had been raised frequently. Clive noticed that he was also dealing with a number of endings in his client work, and the process of managing termination in supervision was assisting him to reflect on his counselling relationships. Karen also encouraged Clive to consider who his new supervisor would be. He was reluctant to do this initially, wanting to 'hold on' to Karen for as long as he could. In their final session together they agreed to each bring a letter, which they read aloud, expressing their feelings about what they had learned from the relationship and what they would take away from supervision. Both found the session very emotional, and tears were shed. As he got up to leave, Clive turned and said: *If it doesn't work out with my new supervisor, can I come back to you?*

Each relationship demonstrates a different 'ending' scenario. In the case of Mark and Bridget, both are initially shocked to learn that supervision will be coming to an end, but they do, at least, have a few sessions left to prepare themselves for the termination. The final session provides an opportunity to celebrate what has been achieved as well as acknowledge the feelings of sadness they are both experiencing at the end of the supervisory relationship. Closure has been achieved for both: Mark can begin work with a new supervisee and Bridget with a new supervisor, having reflected on how much they have learned from each other.

The case of Fran and Gemma is more problematic. Although Fran suspected that her supervisee was struggling with both counselling and supervision, she was still shocked when Gemma announced that she was giving up her counsellor training. Thus Fran was surprised to find out that this was their final session together, and the ending could not, therefore, be planned. Furthermore, Gemma left the session before it concluded, walking out of the relationship, clearly in distress. Fran was left with conflicting emotions: sadness, frustration, anger, self-doubt and relief. She considered contacting her own supervisor to talk through what had happened – something she rarely did outside of designated supervision sessions. But as she reached for the phone, she reflected on the parallel process and pondered how many unplanned endings she had experienced in her counselling practice. This helped her to gain a perspective on what had happened, and she decided to wait until her next supervision session before she spoke to her supervisor. Instead, she called Gemma's placement manager at the college to explain what had happened. Gemma kept to her decision not to continue with her counselling training, although she did not rule out the possibility of returning at some point in the future. She knew that the supervision process had played a significant part in helping her to acknowledge that counselling, at this point in her life, was not for her.

Karen and Clive enjoyed a planned ending to their supervisory relationship as they had six months to prepare for the termination. They used the time well; in particular, it gave Clive the opportunity to reflect further on endings in counselling relationships with clients. The final session was used creatively and provided a safe space in which both could share their feelings about ending and celebrate what they had learned in the relationship. However, Clive's parting question about 'coming back' left Karen feeling anxious. She was worried that her response at the time (a laugh) could have been interpreted by Clive as an agreement to see him again in a supervisory relationship at some point in the future. She decided to speak to her supervisor about what had happened and considered writing to Clive to clarify the situation.

CHAPTER SUMMARY

This chapter focused on the ending stage of supervision. It explored:

- the purpose of review during the supervisory relationship;
- the meaning of 'endings' in the supervisory relationship;
- how to manage the process of termination in supervision effectively;
- the concept of 'new beginnings' and the importance of using the ending of supervision as a starting point for 'moving on'.

Chapters 5 to 9 have explored the stages through which the supervision relationship develops. An effective relationship between supervisor and supervisee serves to illuminate and strengthen counselling practice, develop skills, knowledge and expertise for both parties and attend to the emotional and psychological needs of the supervisee. As in counselling, the relationship, it could be argued, is 'all' (Weaks, 2002).

Finally in this chapter, and particularly in the final case studies, reference has been made to the need for supervisors to use their own supervision effectively. The concept of supervision for the supervisor will be discussed more fully in the next chapter.

SUGGESTED FURTHER READING

Copeland, S (2005) *Counselling supervision in organisations.* London: Routledge.

Chapter 11 deals with endings and new beginnings in supervision.

CHAPTER 10

Supervising the supervisor – transforming counselling practice

Jane Westergaard

CORE KNOWLEDGE

This chapter will provide the opportunity to:

- consider issues raised in supervision;
- identify strategies for supporting the supervisor;
- reflect on the place of research in supporting continuing professional development;
- examine findings from a recent research project with supervisors;
- consider ways in which effective supervisory practice can be disseminated.

INTRODUCTION

Part One of this book has provided an introduction to the key theories, concepts, skills and approaches underpinning supervisory practice, and Part Two has followed the development of the relationship between supervisor and supervisee. So far, attention has been focused on the activity of supervision as it relates to practising counsellors, acknowledging the need to support counsellors in order to ensure effective work with clients. But what about the supervisors themselves? While they are focused on ensuring that they meet the needs of their supervisees, who is supporting them? Here we attempt to address that question and explore supervision from an alternative perspective: that of the supervisor – as supervisee.

The chapter begins by identifying a range of broad areas in which supervisors may require support. It goes on to consider ways in which those support needs can be met, before establishing the place of research in the continuing professional development of supervisors within counselling and the broader helping professions. The chapter concludes by introducing a recent research project with new supervisors who talked about their experiences of supervision with their own supervisors. Overall, the chapter offers the opportunity to consider how effective supervisory practice can be taken forward: how best practice can be disseminated and how supervisors can play an active part in transforming counselling work.

ISSUES AND SUPPORT NEEDS FACED BY SUPERVISORS

There is a well-known expression 'A problem shared is a problem halved', and in many ways, at a very basic level, this sums up the process of both counselling and supervision. As a practising counsellor, I look forward to supervision not only because it offers me a reflective learning space, but also because it provides an environment in which I can be open and honest about my thoughts and feelings concerning my client work. I often find myself approaching supervision sessions with a sense of heaviness, particularly when I am exposed to, or am 'containing' challenging or painful client material. I will frequently leave my supervision sessions with a lighter tread, a feeling that I have 'let go' of the burden – or rather that my supervisor is sharing the load with me. Having undertaken research with counsellors, I know I am not alone in these perceptions. On reflection, this is unsurprising. How many times have clients left counselling saying *I feel so much better now I've told you about this*, while I exit the counselling room bearing the weight of what my client has shared with me?

The parallels between the activities of counselling and supervision are, as always, striking. And the concept of the parallel process has featured throughout this book, in particular when referring to the way in which the relationship between client and counsellor is mirrored or 'paralleled' in the supervisory relationship. Knowledge of this process is helpful for both supervisor and supervisee, as exploring the dynamic in the supervisory relationship often serves to illuminate client practice. So if my clients leave their counselling sessions feeling lighter, and I, in turn, feel the weight of responsibility for sharing their burden, how might my supervisor feel when I 'unload' this material in supervision? And, more importantly, how is my supervisor supported to 'hold' or manage those feelings?

Before we examine the support mechanisms available to supervisors, it is helpful to take a moment to consider the range of issues and challenges that supervisors may face in their supervisory practice.

REFLECTION POINT

List as many potential issues, difficulties and challenges that supervisors may encounter in their work as you can. Think broadly. For example, what issues might be raised when supervising a counsellor in training? What about supervising counsellors who work with children, young people or vulnerable adults? What about those who are training to be supervisors?

In Case study 10.1, Joy, an experienced supervisor, responds to the question *What kind of challenges and issues have you faced as a supervisor?*

Case study 10.1 Joy: supervisor

Wow! That's a big question. Let me think . . . gosh, that really is a big question . . . I suppose when I think about it . . . There are so many things . . . but . . . I guess . . . hmm . . . when I really think about the question, it helps me to reflect on the challenges in relation to the functions. Let me explain what I mean.

I've supervised a number of counsellors now. Some of these have worked in the bereavement counselling agency where I'm employed as a supervisor, and some are counsellors who work in a range of different contexts in private practice. If I think about the kinds of things that come up – the times where I've been stopped in my tracks, the critical incidents, if you like – they can all be framed within the three functions of supervision.

For example, if we take the normative function first – you know, ensuring that counsellors are working within the law and maintaining best practice – I can think of an example, in my private practice, of a counsellor who did not share my own view that the child she was counselling was at risk of significant harm. My supervisee did not want to formally report the case to the appropriate authority, and I was left with high levels of anxiety concerning the welfare of the child. That's one example, but there are plenty more that fall within the normative remit, when counsellors are working close to the boundary of organisational policies and, sometimes, the law.

Second, there's the formative function – particularly where I'm working with new or trainee counsellors and a clear training issue has arisen. Sometimes it can be hard to encourage a supervisee to reflect on areas that require development when they are feeling vulnerable, anxious and defensive about their abilities as a counsellor. Alternatively, I find it just as difficult when supervisees look to me to provide them with answers. Somehow, I never quite feel 'good enough' and I have to constantly struggle with feelings of inadequacy.

Finally, the restorative function has given me some challenging moments too. Sitting alongside a supervisee who is struggling emotionally with the work or experiencing their own pain as a result of issues that have arisen in counselling can be really challenging. Providing the right amount of support without crossing the boundary into therapy is a tough call. And I know I haven't always got it right.

So, in a nutshell, I'd say that I'm constantly being challenged as a supervisor. I'm always asking myself questions about my practice; and those questions relate to ensuring that counsellors are working lawfully and ethically, that they are developing their practice and using supervision as a learning environment and that I am supporting their emotional and psychological well-being. Thank heavens I have my own supervisor to help me make sense of some of this stuff.

Joy suggests a helpful framework to consider the challenges she faces as a supervisor. By reflecting on the three key functions of supervision, she has identified examples of issues she has faced that have challenged her practice as a supervisor. Further examples are outlined below.

Normative function

- Supervisees who overstep the boundaries of their counselling contract with clients.
- Supervisees who present ethical dilemmas in supervision.
- Supervisees who collude with clients who are in danger themselves or are putting others at risk.
- Supervisees who breach the policy of the organisation for which they are working.

Formative function

- Supervisees who do not accept that elements of their practice require development.
- Supervisees who agree to develop their practice but who make no move to do so.
- Supervisees who refuse to conceptualise their work using theoretical frameworks and take an 'I know what works best' approach to working with clients.
- Supervisees who lack insight and empathy.

Restorative function

- Supervisees who are overwhelmed by the emotional demands of the work.
- Supervisees who are dealing with their own challenging emotional issues.
- Supervisees who see supervision as their own therapy.
- Supervisees who deny that the work is having an emotional impact on them.

Of course, these are not full and comprehensive lists, but they do raise a number of challenges that supervisors may face, and, as Joy points out strongly, they suggest that supervisors, like counsellors, are likely to need support themselves in order to manage the complexities of the work.

In a survey of supervisors (Wheeler and King, 2001), 90 per cent of those who responded confirmed that they received supervision themselves, and when asked to identify the key issues that they discussed with their supervisor, the results were compiled under six headings.

- Ethical issues – for example, whether or not supervisees attend for supervision and their fitness to practice.
- Boundaries – helping supervisees to set and keep boundaries with clients.
- Competence – voicing concerns about supervisees' competence as counsellors.
- Training – identifying training opportunities and needs.
- Contracts – ensuring that both counselling and supervision contracts are in place and adhered to.
- Supervisee/client relationship – exploring aspects of their supervisee's counselling practice with specific clients.

The categories identified above 'fit' within the normative, formative and restorative functions – and, interestingly, the normative is emphasised. The research highlights both the issues that supervisors take to their supervision and the importance of supervision for the supervisors. Furthermore, the need for supervision is confirmed by the majority of the research respondents, who stated that even if supervision was not a requirement of the BACP, they would continue to access support. What, then, do the BACP regulations say about supervision for supervisors and what might this supervision look like?

SUPPORTING THE SUPERVISOR

The BACP states in its ethical framework that *all counsellors, psychotherapists, trainers and supervisors are required to have regular and on-going formal supervision/consultative support for their work in accordance with professional requirements* (2010, p6). So supervisors, like counsellors, are required to receive supervision and engage in other forms of support and self-development activity. And, like counsellors, this supervision (and support) can come in a variety of forms. We will investigate the wider support mechanisms further later. But first, how, if at all, is supervision for the supervisor different from supervision for the counsellor?

As already stated, in many ways the process of supervising the supervisors mirrors that of supervising counsellors. But instead of using the time to focus on work with clients, supervisors will share their experiences as supervisors; in effect, the supervisee replaces the client in these supervision sessions. And so the process is paralleled one stage further, with discussions between the supervisor and their supervisor shedding light on the work between the supervisor and counsellor, which, in turn, serves to illuminate the counselling relationship.

ACTIVITY 10.1

Imagine a supervision session between a supervisor and their supervisor and a session between a supervisor and a counsellor. The parallels are clear, but what are the differences? Note down the difference in focus between the two activities.

Clearly there are broad similarities between the role of supervisor to counsellors and the practice of supervising the supervisor. But, as you will probably have noted, there are some differences too. Wheeler and King offer a helpful summary of what constitutes supervision for the supervisor:

> The consultant supervisor provides support and space for reflection, but cannot be held responsible for the work of either the counsellor or the supervisor. They have a moral responsibility to the profession that could result in action under exceptional circumstances. They have a duty of care to the supervisors they work with to have an eye to their safety and wellbeing and to encourage practitioners to work within the limits of their own competence. The consultant is responsible for deciding how they should focus their attention in the sessions, which might ensure that the supervisor's internal supervisor does the majority of the work, processing material and subsequently making decisions that rightfully belong to them.
>
> (Wheeler and King, 2001, p176)

Use of the expression 'consultant supervisor' suggests a subtle shift in emphasis between the role of supervising the counsellor and that of acting as consultant to the supervisor. The focus is on enabling the supervisor to 'process material' and 'make decisions' in the capacity of consultant. In many ways, the relationship reflects the working alliance stage of the supervisory relationship introduced in Chapter 8. Although it is true to say that the similarities outnumber the differences between the role of supervisor and consultant supervisor, it is nevertheless important to be aware of the boundaries of the role as outlined above.

The methods used to supervise supervisors also parallel those used in counsellor supervision. These methods are examined in Chapter 4, and could include individual supervision – with a line manager, a colleague within the organisation or an external supervisor – and group supervision – facilitated by an experienced supervisor or peer group supervision.

In addition to supervision, there are other sources of support and development available to supervisors to ensure that they keep their practice well honed and continue to enhance their knowledge and skills.

ACTIVITY 10.2

As well as supervision with a consultant supervisor, identify the support mechanisms, networks and methods that a supervisor might access to ensure their own continuing professional development.

It is likely that your list included a range of individuals, agencies, training opportunities, therapeutic support and research projects that might be available to ensure that supervisors continue to develop their personal and professional lives. Despenser makes a helpful point about the importance of building networks in counselling practice. Her words can also be applied to supervisors:

> *Therapists should not place total reliance on formal supervision as the only source of support, information and knowledge for themselves and their work. Good reflective practitioners also take responsibility for developing a Referral Resource network of people who can provide them (in confidence) with specialist knowledge and information when they need it.*
>
> (2009, p2)

Supervisors should, therefore, take the opportunity to build their own resources, which will, in many ways, reflect the contexts in which they are supervising. For example, those who supervise addiction counsellors are likely to have access to different resources and networks to those who supervise counsellors who work with children. And 'resources' should not only include people and organisations who can offer information, advice and guidance, but also the literature, which is wide-ranging and up to date and often draws on recent research in order to promote and disseminate best practice. For example, the BACP circulates a quarterly journal to its members – *Counselling and Psychotherapy Research* – which reports on the latest research and developments in counselling and supervision practice.

Joy – who shared her thoughts earlier when questioned about the challenges she faces as a supervisor – goes on to talk about the ways in which she receives support to enable her to manage and develop her supervision practice.

Case study 10.2 Joy: supervisor

As I said earlier, my own supervision is really important in supporting me with my work as a supervisor. I don't know what I'd do without it! I see my own supervisor regularly, but I also meet with the line manager in the counselling agency where I supervise.

She's great! She has loads of experience and expertise about the client group with whom the counsellors work, and I draw on her knowledge all the time. Every month, all the supervisors in the agency also meet together for peer supervision. I find this really useful too, in terms of sharing best practice and getting support from my colleagues.

I do other stuff as well to try to improve and develop my practice. Whenever training opportunities arise, I try to take them. I can't go on all the courses that I find out about, but the agency is very good in sharing the cost with me if I find something that appeals and is considered relevant to my work. I also read what I can, mainly by accessing the journals – The Clinical Supervisor *often has really interesting articles that I can reflect on in relation to my own practice.*

I take my work seriously and try to improve as best I can. My line manager asked me if I would consider writing something myself for publication in the counselling agency newsletter. I agreed . . . but feel nervous about it. This isn't something I've done before, but I do believe that it's important.

Joy refers to a range of support opportunities that she accesses in order to reflect on and develop her work as a supervisor. As expected, Joy mentions the people who support her directly – her line manager and her peers, as well as other agencies and networks that can offer guidance. She also makes reference to the literature and, in particular, the part that research findings, reported in journals, play in furthering her knowledge. Joy also demonstrates that she is willing to disseminate her own ideas and practice by writing for her agency's publication.

Every profession or academic discipline is dependent on research to ensure that practice is continually improving and that evidence is gathered to support the work and help to transform the practitioners' (and clients') experience. Often, professional journals will publish findings from research projects that have been undertaken in the field; and the counselling profession depends on high-quality research – both qualitative and quantitative – to enhance its service. The need for continuing professional development for supervisors and the progression of the wider practice of counselling and supervision should provide opportunities for practitioners to become involved in research into aspects of the profession. What follows is an introduction to a research study conducted with supervisors in order to reflect on and evaluate aspects of their supervision practice.

RESEARCH WITH SUPERVISORS: PROCESS AND FINDINGS

McLeod, writing about counselling research, suggests that those involved in the counselling profession are reluctant to engage in research, assuming that the activity is *about numbers, impenetrable statistics and large samples and has no place for ordinary human feelings and experiences* (1994, p4). He goes on to suggest that this assumption is ill-perceived and that, in fact, counsellors (and supervisors) engage constantly in research in their counselling sessions, in their reflections, through their training and in supervision. He suggests this definition of research: *a systematic process of critical enquiry leading to valid propositions and conclusions that are communicated to interested others* (1994, p4).

> ## REFLECTION POINT
>
> Think about your practice – either as a supervisor or a counsellor. Bearing in mind the definition of research outlined above, can you identify ways in which you are already involved in critical enquiry that you share with interested others – and which is, therefore, by implication, research?

This reflection may seem daunting at first glance. However, it is likely that you reflected on both counselling and supervision as examples of research activity. Sharing counselling experiences in supervision or with a peer group can constitute research as outlined in the definition above. McLeod makes the point that research should not only refer to formal projects carried out by academics but should also be a more accessible and ongoing process.

What follows is an introduction to a research project undertaken with supervisors feeding back and evaluating key findings relating to their experiences as supervisors. In particular, the research raises interesting issues related to supervising the supervisors that are worthy of reflection.

The research project

The research project focused on the experiences of five supervisors employed in an agency that offers support to children and young people at risk of exclusion from school. I had met the participants a year before undertaking the research, in my capacity as a teacher in higher education, where they were studying on an accredited supervision training programme. I was curious at the time about the levels of anxiety among students who were enrolled on the course. The main reason for this, it transpired, was that the students, although employed by their organisation at the time as line managers, would soon be taking on responsibility for the supervision of colleagues whom they also line-managed. In the past, their colleagues had been supervised by external supervisors. A year later, I returned to explore their experiences of the dual role – taking on the supervision of colleagues, while at the same time line-managing them. In this particular piece of research, I was less concerned with finding out about a specific, pre-determined (by me) aspect of the participants' experiences; rather, through a process of individual interviews (recorded, transcribed and analysed), I invited each participant to tell me, in their own words, about their experience of supervision.

A number of shared themes – as well as individual issues – emerged. The shared themes were:

- the challenges of line-manager supervision;
- managing supervisees' resistance to receiving line-manager supervision;
- the need for supervision in the 'helping professions';
- supervision for the supervisors.

Sadly, space here does not allow for a full analysis of each theme. Instead, in keeping with the focus of this chapter, what follows are the participants' responses to the last point – their own support and supervision.

Research findings

The participants in the study provide line-management supervision, and, in turn, their own consultant supervisors are also their line managers. Much has been written about the tension between line management and supervision (Nixon and Carroll, 1994; Page and Woskett, 1994; Copeland, 2001; Edwards, 2001), and this supervision method is one that most counsellors do not experience.

The pros and cons of line-management supervision were discussed in Chapter 4. Although the BACP is not in favour of this method, a number of counsellors (and others who use counselling skills in their work in the broader remit of the helping professions) receive supervision from their line managers. Edwards (2001) takes a contrasting view, pointing out that line managers have a legitimate interest in their colleagues' work and should therefore have the opportunity to attend to issues raised in supervision.

In this research project, the supervisors, although expressing reservations about their dual role as line managers and supervisors, were all positive about the relationships they had formed with their colleagues as supervisees. That said, where participants talked about their supervision with their own line managers, it was clear that in most cases the process was not paralleled – the reasons for this will be explored later.

It should be noted that in the examples that follow, all the names of participants have been changed to ensure anonymity. Belinda explains:

I still feel that we don't have the real supervisory space because our sessions with our line managers are always supervision/line management and we only have, um, maybe half an hour. And so within that, what we tend to be talking about is the relationship between me and my supervisee, not necessarily the client at the bottom.

Jocelyn agrees:

My line manager is good. But because of the demands of the job, it's not always possible to focus on, you know, my supervisees.

Junior echoes this view:

Supervision with my line-manager . . . well sometimes it doesn't happen because other things, you know, more important things take priority in the day-to-day business of the organisation. It tends to be more challenging and less nurturing, which I suppose is not necessarily a bad thing.

Bethany explains how she seeks support beyond supervision with her line manager:

I think probably through talking through the tensions and issues with my colleagues, I've got support that way. And it's not because my line manager isn't open to that, it's just that often line management is about the targets and the work we're doing and we don't always have the space to really deal with issues in depth.

REFLECTION POINT

So far, what do the participants' responses tell us about the widely held view that the duality of line management and supervision can be problematic?

Interestingly, as explained earlier, the participants did not share these negative feelings about their own dual role as line-managers and supervisors. Jocelyn talks about this from her perspective as line manager/supervisor:

I was excited because for me it's all about the work and I didn't really like the idea of not knowing what my practitioners were doing in their work with children and families. I felt quite detached from it and very uncomfortable. I was pleased that I was able to be a bit more 'hands on' and be able to benefit from listening to my supervisees.

Charlie explains how becoming a supervisor has had a positive impact on his line management style:

I'm probably a bit gentler than I was, focusing a little bit more on the holistic, you know, the practitioner as a whole. I've become increasingly aware that my practitioners have skills, you know, they know things that I don't. It's more of a working partnership, you know, learning from each other.

Belinda concurred, and expressed surprise to find that the line-manager model has worked well for her supervisees:

I would say that I'm not so anti line-management supervision as I was. I feel that even though it's been tricky, it kind of has worked. Whether that is because I'm particularly non-authoritarian as a manager, I don't know.

But she went on to say:

Probably the best way would be having a supervisor who is a line manager, but not the supervisee's line manager.

REFLECTION POINT

Why might the participants feel that the dual role works well in their position as line managers and supervisors, whereas, as suggested earlier, they do not view it as effective in their own supervision with their line managers?

One possible answer to this question lies in the perception among the participants that they had little confidence in their line managers as supervisors because although the participants themselves had received supervision training their line-managers had not. Charlie explains:

My own supervision with my line-manager is not mirrored in terms of the way I supervise. The philosophy of the supervision training . . . well . . . it's just not mirrored in my own supervision.

Jocelyn agrees:

I do speak to my supervisor about things. But this is where I have a slight problem. I don't want to put the blame on anyone, but I struggle with my own supervisor because she didn't have the training I did. In some ways she reminds me of myself before I had the supervision training.

Belinda went further:

I didn't trust her at all to begin with. I was angry because she hadn't gone through the same training that I had, so I felt if I wanted to talk about a theory or something I was worried about, then there wasn't anybody to share this with.

The issue of lack of training for the participants' line managers was echoed by all who took part in the research. It suggests that in order to build an effective, trusting supervisory relationship, there has to be confidence in the skills and knowledge of the supervisor to carry out the role.

We have seen a small sample of the rich data that the research produced. A full analysis is published in *The Clinical Supervisor* (Westergaard, 2012). What is clear from what we have read is that the aim of research is to illuminate and inform practice. It is not undertaken in a vacuum – nor is it only for the eyes of academics. Research alongside other professional development activities can and should assist to inform and develop practice at every level.

So in order that supervisors are supported to develop their practice, they should take advantage of a full range of professional development activities. These include:

- supervision;
- peer support;
- training;
- networks – including other agencies/individuals;
- literature – journals and other recent publications;
- research – either their own, which can be disseminated, or as part of an external project.

ACTIVITY 10.3

Take a moment now to reflect on your own professional development as a supervisor. Begin by writing down the support that you currently access. Then make a list of other forms of support that you are aware of but do not access regularly. From this list, complete an action plan that sets out your thoughts regarding your own development over the next year. What would you like to work on? How can you be supported to do this? And finally, how might you share your new knowledge and expertise with others?

The final question in the activity above is important. If we are to continue to learn and develop, we also need to be prepared to share our experiences, knowledge and skills with others. This can be done in a number of ways including:

- sharing experience and practice with peers;
- taking issues to managers, where appropriate;

- using supervision to share experiences and develop knowledge and skills;
- writing and disseminating reports;
- undertaking and publishing research.

CHAPTER SUMMARY

This chapter has:

- considered a range of issues raised in supervision and reflected on the support needs encountered by supervisors;
- identified various strategies that can help to support supervisors;
- encouraged reflection on the place of research in supporting continuing professional development in counselling and supervision;
- examined findings from a recent research project involving supervisors;
- considered ways in which effective supervisory practice can be disseminated.

CONCLUSION

To conclude, this book began by introducing key theories and concepts underpinning supervision practice and it went on to explore the developing relationship between supervisor and supervisee. It has ended by establishing the importance of continuing to develop our professional knowledge and skills in order that our work as supervisors, the practice of those whom we supervise and the experience of our clients in counselling might be transformed.

This book has demonstrated that supervision is both a complex and rewarding practice. In our view, it is part of a process that helps to make counselling ethical, professional and effective. As such, it enables counsellors, therapists and those working in the helping professions to achieve knowledgeable practice based on insights derived from reflexive and creative approaches in theory and in practice. Our experience, our reading and research, and the writing of this text have helped us to understand the practice further. We hope our book aids your understanding of supervision.

SUGGESTED FURTHER READING

Bradley, L and **Ladany, N** (2001) *Counselor supervision: principles, process and practice.* Philadelphia PA: Brunner-Routledge.

Chapter 12 focuses on undertaking research in supervision.

Wheeler, S and **King, D** (2001) *Supervising counsellors: issues of responsibility.* London: Sage.

Chapter 10 provides a helpful introduction to supervising the supervisors.

The Clinical Supervisor

A key journal for supervisors – includes articles on practice and research papers.

References

Argyris, C and Schön, D (1996) *Organisational learning II: theory, method and practice.* Wokingham: Addison-Wesley.

Arkin, N, Freund, A and Saltman, I (1999) A group supervision model for broadening multiple-method skills of social work students. *Social Work Education,* 18, 1: 49–58.

BAC (British Association for Counselling) (1988) *Code of ethics and practice for the supervision of counsellors.* Rugby: BAC.

BACP (British Association for Counselling and Psychotherapy) (2010) *Ethical framework for good practice in counselling and psychotherapy.* Lutterworth: BACP.

Bamber, J (1998) Learning, understanding and the development of critical practice. *Youth & Policy,* 60: 30–45.

Banks, S (2009) From professional ethics to ethics in professional life: implications for learning, teaching and study. *Ethics and Social Welfare,* 3, 1: 55–63.

Barden, N (2001) The responsibility of the supervisor in the British Association for Counselling & Psychotherapy's codes of ethics and practice, in Wheeler, S and King, D (eds) *Supervising counsellors: issues of responsibility.* London: Sage.

Berne, E (1964) *Games people play.* Harmondsworth: Penguin.

Bimrose, J (2006) Multicultural issues in support and supervision, in Reid, H L and Westergaard, J (eds) *Providing support and supervision: an introduction for professionals working with young people.* Abingdon: Routledge.

Bond, T and Mitchels, B (2008) *Confidentiality and record keeping in counselling and psychotherapy.* London: Sage and BACP.

Boud, D, Keogh, R and Walker, D (1985) *Reflection: turning experience into learning.* London: Routledge.

Bradley, L J, Kottler, J A and Lehrman-Waterman, D (2001) Ethical issues in supervision, in Bradley, L J and Ladany, N (eds) *Counselor supervision: principles, process and practice.* Philadelphia PA: Brunner-Routledge.

Breene, C (2011) Resistance is a natural path: an alternative perspective on transformation, in Shohet, R (ed.) *Supervision as transformation: a passion for learning.* London: Jessica Kingsley.

Brockbank, A and McGill, I (2007) *Facilitating reflective learning in higher education,* 2nd edition. Maidenhead: McGraw-Hill, SRHE/Open University Press.

Burr, V (1995) *An introduction to social constructivism.* London: Routledge.

Carroll, M (1996) *Counselling supervision: theory, skills and practice.* London: Continuum.

Claringbull, N (2010) *What is counselling & psychotherapy?* Exeter: Learning Matters.

Copeland, S (2001) Supervisor responsibility within organizational contents, in Wheeler, S and King, D (eds) *Supervising counselors: issues of responsibility.* London: Sage.

Copeland, S (2005) *Counselling supervision in organisations.* London: Routledge.

Corey, G, Corey, M S and Callanan, P (1993) *Issues and ethics in the helping professions,* 4th edition. Pacific Grove CA: Brooks/Cole.

Cribb, A and Ball, S (2005) Towards an ethical audit of the privatisation of education. *British Journal of Educational Studies,* 53, 2, June 2005: 115–28.

Daniels, D and Jenkins, P (2010) *Therapy with children: children's rights, confidentiality and the law,* 2nd edition. London: Sage.

d'Ardenne, P and Mahtani, A (1989) *Transcultural counselling in action.* London: Sage.

Davis, D D (2008) *Terminating therapy: a professional guide to ending on a positive note.* New York: Wiley.

Davys, A and Beddoe, L (2010) *Best practice in professional supervision: a guide for the helping professions.* London: Jessica Kingsley.

Despenser, S (2009) Getting the most from supervision. *Therapy Today* 20, 8: 28–31.

DoH (Department of Health) (2003) *The Victoria Climbié Inquiry, Lord Laming.* London: HMSO.

Dryden, W (2008) *Key issues for counselling in action.* London: Sage.

Dryden, W, Horton, I and Mearns, D (1995) *Issues in professional counsellor training*. London: Cassell.

Edwards, A (2001) Developing a framework for support for personal advisers, in Edwards, A (ed.) *Supporting personal advisers in Connexions: perspectives on supervision and mentoring from allied professions*. Occasional Paper. Centre for Career & Personal Development, Canterbury Christ Church University College.

Egan, G (2007) *The skilled helper: a problem-management and opportunity-development approach to helping*, 8th edition. Pacific Grove CA: Brooks/Cole.

Ellis, M V and Ladany, N (1997) Inferences concerning supervisees and clients in clinical supervision: an integrative review, in Watkins, C E (ed.) *Handbook of Psychotherapy Supervision*. New York: Wiley.

Embleton, G (2002) Dangerous liaisons and shifting boundaries in psychoanalytic perspectives on supervision, in McMahon, M and Patton, W (eds) *Supervision in the helping professions: a practical approach*. Frenchs Forest, Australia: Pearson Education.

Feltham, C (2002a) Supervision: a surveillance culture? *Counselling & Psychotherapy Journal*, February 2002: 26–27.

Feltham, C (2002b) Supervision: critical issues to be faced from the beginning, in McMahon, M and Patton, W (eds) *Supervision in the helping professions, a practical approach*. Frenchs Forest, Australia: Pearson Education.

Feltham, C and Dryden, W (1994) *Developing counsellor supervision*. London: Sage.

Foucault, M (1979) *Discipline and punish: the birth of the prison*. Sheridan, A (trans). London: Tavistock.

Gillick v West Norfolk Area Health Authority (1985) at 420. London: HMSO.

Green, J (2010) *Creating the therapeutic relationship in counselling and psychotherapy*. Exeter: Learning Matters.

Harris, M and Brockbank, A (2011) *An integrative approach to therapy and supervision: a practical guide for counsellors and psychotherapists*. London: Jessica Kingsley Publishers.

Hawkins, P and Shohet, R (1989) *Supervision in the helping professions*. Milton Keynes: Open University Press.

Hawkins, P and Shohet, R (2006) *Supervision in the helping professions* (3rd edition). Maidenhead: Open University Press.

Heron, J (1975) *Six category intervention analysis*. Guildford: University of Surrey.

Hewson, J (1999) Training supervisors to contract in supervision, in Holloway, E and Carroll, M (eds) *Training counselling supervisors*. London: Sage.

Holloway, E L (1995) *Clinical supervision: a systems approach*. Thousand Oaks CA: Sage.

Holloway, E (1997) Structures for the analysis of teaching and supervision, in Watkins, C E (ed.) *Handbook of psychotherapy supervision*. Hoboken NJ: John Wiley and Sons Ltd.

Holloway, E L and Aposhyan, H M (1994) The supervisor as teacher, model, and mentor for careers and psychotherapy. *Journal of Career Assessment*, 2, 2, Spring: 191–97.

Holloway, E and Carroll, M (eds) (1999) *Training counselling supervisors*. London: Sage.

Horton, I (2012) Integration, in Feltham, C and Horton, I (eds) *The Sage handbook of counselling and psychotherapy*. London: Sage.

Hughes, L and Pengelly, P (1997) *Staff supervision in a turbulent environment: managing process and task in front-line services*. London: Jessica Kingsley.

Inskipp, F and Proctor, B (1993) *The art, craft and tasks of counselling supervision, Part 1: making the most of supervisors*. Twickenham: Cascade Publications.

Inskipp, F and Proctor, B (2009) *Making the most of supervision*, 2nd edition. Twickenham: Cascade.

Jenkins, P (2001) Supervisory responsibility and the law, in Wheeler, S and King, D (eds) *Supervising counsellors: issues of responsibility*. London: Sage.

Kadushin, A (1976) *Supervision in social work*. New York: Columbia University Press.

Kazdin, A E (1996) Dropping out of child psychotherapy: issues for research and implications for practice. *Clinical Child Psychology and Psychiatry*, 1: 133–56.

Knight, J (2003) Reflections on the therapist-supervisor relationship, in Wiener, J, Mizen, R and Duckham, J (eds) *Supervising and being supervised: a practice in search of a theory*. Basingstoke: Palgrave Macmillan.

Kolb, D (1984) *Experiential learning*. Englewood Cliffs NJ: Prentice Hall.

Lawton, B and Feltham, C (2000) Counselling supervision baselines, problems and possibilities, in Lawton, B and Feltham, C (eds) *Taking supervision forward*. London: Sage.

Lizzio, A and Wilson, K (2002) The domain of learning goals in professional supervision, in McMahon, M and Patton, W (eds) *Supervision in the helping professions: a practical approach*. Frenchs Forest, Australia: Pearson Education.

Luft, J (1984) *Group process: an introduction to group dynamics,* 2nd edition. Mountain View CA: Mayfield Publishing.

Mander, G (2000) Beginnings, endings and outcomes: a comparison of methods and goals. *Psychodynamic Counselling,* 6, 3: 301–17.

McCulloch, K (2007) Ethics, accountability and the shaping of youth work practice, in Harrison, R, Benjamin, C, Curran, S and Hunter, R (eds) *Leading work with young people.* London: Sage/Open University.

McLeod, J (1994) *Doing counselling research.* London: Sage.

McLeod, J (1998) *An introduction to counselling,* 2nd edition. Buckingham: Open University Press.

McMahon, M (2002) Some supervision practicalities, in McMahon, M and Patton, W (eds) *Supervision in the helping professions: a practical approach.* Frenchs Forest, Australia: Pearson Education.

McMahon, M and Patton, W (2000) Conversations on clinical supervision: benefits perceived by school counsellors. *British Journal of Guidance & Counselling,* 28, 3: 339–51.

Mearns, D (1991) On being a supervisor, in Dryden, W and Thorne, B (eds) *Training and supervision for counselling in action.* London: Sage.

Mearns, D (2008) *How much supervision should you have?* BACP information sheet S1. Lutterworth: BACP.

Mearns, D and Thorne, B (2007) *Person centred counselling in action,* 3rd edition. London: Sage.

Mezirow, J (1994) Understanding transformation theory. *Adult Education Quarterly,* 44, 4: 222–44.

Mitchels, B and Bond, T (2010) *Essential law for counsellors and psychotherapists.* London: Sage and BACP.

Morrissette, P J (2002) *Self-supervision: a primer for counselors and helping professionals.* New York: Brunner-Routledge.

Murdin, L (2000) *How much is enough? Endings in psychotherapy and counselling.* London: Routledge.

Muse-Burke, J L, Ladany, N and Deck, M D (2001) The supervisory relationship, in Bradley, L J and Ladany, N (eds) *Counsellor supervision: principles, process and practice.* Hove: Brunner-Routledge.

Nelson-Jones, R (2012) *Basic counselling skills: a helper's manual.* London: Sage.

Nixon, J and Carroll, M (1994). Can a line manager also be a counselor? *Employee Counselling Today,* 6, 1: 10–15.

Page, S and Woskett, V (1994) *Supervising the counsellor: a cyclical model.* London: Routledge.

Page, S and Wosket, V (2001) *Supervising the counsellor: a cyclical model,* 2nd edition. Philadelphia PA: Brunner-Routledge.

Parker, I (2007) *Revolution in psychology: alienation to emancipation.* London: Pluto Press.

Perls, F (1972) *Gestalt therapy.* Moab UT: Real People Press.

Prever, M (2010) *Counselling and supporting children and young people: a person-centred approach.* London: Sage.

Rapisarda, C A, Desmond, K J and Nelson, J R (2011) Student reflections on the journey to being a supervisor. *The Clinical Supervisor,* 30, 1: 109–23.

Reid, H L (2004) Jiminy Cricket on my shoulder: professional common sense and formal supervision as routes to ethical watchfulness for personal advisers, in Reid, H L and Bimrose, J (eds) *Constructing the future: reflection on practice.* Stourbridge: Institute of Career Guidance.

Reid, H L (2006) What is support and supervision? in Reid, H L and Westergaard, J (eds) *Providing support and supervision: an introduction for professionals working with young people.* London: Routledge.

Reid, H L (2007a) The shaping of discourse positions in the development of support and supervision for personal advisers in England. *British Journal of Guidance & Counselling,* 35, 1: 59–78.

Reid, H L (2007b) Structuring support and supervision for different contexts, in Harrison, R, Benjamin, C, Curran, S and Hunter, R (eds) *Leading work with young people.* London: Sage/Open University.

Reid, H L (2010) Supervision to enhance educational and vocational guidance practice: a review. *International Journal for Vocational & Educational Guidance,* 10, 3: 191–205.

Reid, H L (2011) Embedding multicultural principles and skills into counselling work with young people, in, Reid, H L and Westergaard, J. *Effective counselling with young people.* Exeter: Learning Matters.

Reid, H L and Fielding, A J (2007) *Providing support to young people: a guide to interviewing in helping relationships*. Abingdon: Routledge.

Reid, H L and Westergaard, J (2006) Providing support and supervision: what makes 'good' supervision? in Reid, H L (ed.) *Re-positioning careers education and guidance*. Occasional Paper, Centre for Career and Personal Guidance, Canterbury Christ Church University.

Reynolds, H (2006) Beyond reason and anxiety: how psychoanalytical ideas can inform the practice of supervision, in Reid, H L and Westergaard, J (eds) *Providing support and supervision: an introduction for professionals working with young people*. London: Routledge.

Rogers, C R (1951) *Client centred therapy*. Boston MA: Houghton Mifflin.

Scaife, J (2001) *Supervision in the mental health professions: a practitioner's guide*. Hove: Brunner/Routledge.

Scaife, J (2010) *Supervising the reflective practitioner: an essential guide to theory and practice*. London: Routledge.

Schön, D (1983) *The reflective practitioner*. New York: Basic Books.

Schuck, C and Wood, J (2011) *Inspiring creative supervision*. London: Jessica Kingsley.

Shohet, R (2011) *Supervision as transformation*. London: Jessica Kingsley.

Shohet, R and Wilmot, J (1991) The key issues in the supervision of counsellors, in Dryden, W and Thorne, B (eds) *Training and supervision for counsellors in action*. London: Sage.

Shulman, L (2006) The clinical supervisor–practitioner working alliance. *The Clinical Supervisor*, 24, 1–2: 23.47.

Sterner, W R (2009) Influence of the supervisory working alliance on supervisee work satisfaction and work-related stress. *Journal of Mental Health Counselling*, 31, 3: 249–63.

Stoltenberg, C D (1981) Approaching supervision from a developmental perspective: the counselor complexity model. *Journal of Counseling Psychology*, 28: 59–65.

Stoltenberg, C and Delworth, U (1987) *Supervising counselors and therapists: a developmental approach*. San Francisco CA: Jossey-Bass Wiley.

Stoltenberg, C, McNeill, B and Delworth, U (1998) *IDM Supervision: an integrated developmental model for supervising counselors and therapists*. San Francisco CA: Jossey Bass.

Storey, J and Billingham, J (2001) Occupational stress and social work. *Social Work Education*, 20, 6: 659–70.

Sue, D W, Arrendondon, P and McDavis, R J (1995) Multicultural counseling competencies and standards: a call to the profession, in Ponterotto, J G, Casas, J M, Suzuki, L A and Alexander, C M (eds) *Handbook of multicultural counseling*. Thousand Oaks CA: Sage.

Thompson, N (1993) *Anti-discriminatory practice*. London: Macmillan.

Tudor, K and Sills, C (2012) Transactional analysis, in Feltham, C and Horton, I (eds) *The Sage handbook of counselling and psychotherapy*. London: Sage.

Turner, B (2000) Supervision and mentoring in child and family social work: the role of the first-line manager in the implementation of the post-qualifying framework. *Social Work Education*, 19, 3: 231–40.

Wall, J C (1994) Teaching termination to trainees through parallel process in supervision. *Clinical Supervisor*, 12, 2: 22–37.

Weaks, D (2002) Unlocking the secrets of 'good supervision': a phenomenological exploration of experienced counsellors' perceptions of good supervision. *Counselling and Psychotherapy Research*, 2, 1: 33–39.

Webb, A, and Wheeler, S (1998) How honest do counsellors dare to be in the supervisory relationship? An exploratory study. *British Journal of Guidance & Counselling*, 26, 4: 509–24.

Westergaard, J (2006) Getting the most from support and supervision: attitudes and skills for supervisors and supervisees in an integrative approach to supervision, in Reid, H L and Westergaard, J (eds) *Providing support and supervision: an introduction for professionals working with young people*. London: Routledge.

Westergaard, J (2011) Using transactional analysis to develop effective communication in counselling young people, in Reid, H L and Westergaard, J (eds) *Effective counselling with young people*. Exeter: Learning Matters.

Westergaard, J (2012) Counselling young people: counsellors' perspectives on 'what works': an exploratory study. *Counselling and Psychotherapy Research* (in press).

Westergaard, J (2012) Line management supervision in the helping professions: experiences of clinical supervisors in an organisation moving from external supervision to a line manager supervisor model. *The Clinical Supervisor* (forthcoming).

Wheeler, S and King, D (2001) *Supervising counsellors: issues of responsibility.* London: Sage.

Whiting, P P, Bradley, L J and Planny, K J (2001) Supervision-based developmental models of counsellor supervision, in Bradley, L J and Ladany, N (eds) *Counselor supervision: principles, process and practice.* Philadelphia PA: Brunner-Routledge.

Wiener, J, Mizen, R and Duckham, J (2003) (eds) *Supervising and being supervised: a practice in search of a theory.* Basingstoke: Palgrave Macmillan.

Winnicott, D (1971) *Playing and reality.* London: Routledge.

Wright, M (2004) Supervising school counsellors: a case for specialism? *CP Journal*, BACP, February 2004: 40–41.

Index